NO OTHER GODS

NO OTHER GODS

Christian Belief in Dialogue with
Buddhism, Hinduism, and Islam

by

H. M. VROOM

translated by

Lucy Jansen

WILLIAM B. EERDMANS PUBLISHING COMPANY
GRAND RAPIDS, MICHIGAN / CAMBRIDGE, U.K.

© 1996 Wm. B. Eerdmans Publishing Co.

255 Jefferson Ave. S.E., Grand Rapids, Michigan 49503 /

P.O. Box 163, Cambridge CB3 9BA U.K.

Printed in the United States of America

01 00 99 98 97 96   7 6 5 4 3 2 1

ISBN 0-8028-4097-3

Contents

Preface

The title of this book, *No Other Gods,* can be read in two ways: with an exclamation mark or with a question mark. A question mark — *no other gods?* — might indicate that the book emphasizes the uniqueness of the Christian faith as opposed to other religions: it *does* concern other gods. But an exclamation mark — *no other gods!* — would give it a completely different meaning: then it would imply that all religions deal with the same God. In order to find out whether I intend to have a question mark or an exclamation mark after the title, and whether I believe that only Christians have a monopoly on true belief or that all religions are related, one will need to read this book in its entirety. Even more interesting than my thoughts regarding this, however, is what readers themselves conclude after reading and reflecting on it: Is it a critical question, an exclamation, or, possibly, neither?

This book is more or less a continuation of a broader study on the views of the great religious traditions, their views on truth, and their mutual relationship. In that study I refrained from making any sort of judgment regarding the various insights of belief. Of course, no one who has read all that can avoid the question of what a person himself holds to be true. This book is concerned with *weighing* the views and experiences handed down within four great religious traditions: Christian faith in dialogue with Buddhism, Hinduism, and Islam. The structure of the argumentation here dictates the order of the book as a whole.

The book was written in 1993, the year in which the Parliament of the World's Religions met for the second time in Chicago. The first, held in 1893 in Chicago, met at a time when colonialism flourished and belief in progress held Western thought in its grip.[1] The second Parliament took place in a time in which the evils of a society under the sway of technology and economical life are daily becoming more visible. People who believe have to try to arrive at solutions together and find a way of life that allows people their worth and does no further damage to nature. Mutual understanding, cooperation, and critical dialogue among adherents of the world religions are urgent.

In a short time religious pluralism has developed into one of the most burning questions in society. Religions have been discovered to be of great importance in the transference of norms and values and in the building of civilizations. If people wish to acquire ideals that extend beyond those that concern only their own well-being, then they need a view of people and the world as well as of that which transcends people and the world. But religion also often plays a role in conflicts between nations and groups of people. It is necessary to have an open and honest dialogue on the all-important questions of God, people, and the world, and it is my hope that this book can help.

The first ideas for this book originated from a number of lectures, and were discussed a few years ago with a group of students; I am grateful to them for their critical remarks. Dr. R. Fernhout, Dr. R. Kranenborg, Dr. M. van den Boom, and Dr. A. W. Musschenga were so kind as to read and to comment on, respectively, chapters two, three, four, and five. I thank them for their trouble; they are not responsible for any inaccuracies or oversimplified passages in the text of this book.

1. For a broad selection of articles from the first World's Parliament of Religions, see R. H. Seager, ed., *The Dawn of Religious Pluralism: Voices from the World's Parliament of Religions (1893)* (La Salle: Open Court, 1993).

1

Introduction

Our culture has become pluralistic: Christianity is no longer the dominant belief system. Interest in religion is on the increase again after having declined in the 1970s. This does not mean, however, that people are returning to the same positions as earlier, for there is now a variety of religions to sample. Eastern religions have attracted a great deal of interest. Many people, including Christians, believe in reincarnation, and interest in meditation and spirituality has greatly increased. Due to cultural shifts, the transference of belief within Christian churches has become more problematic. In general, Christians have become more independent; we decide for ourselves what we will believe. We form our own opinions because we reflect deeply about the issues confronting us. We make choices, exposing ourselves to some influences and resisting others. To some extent this is not a matter of choice: we are subject to these influences and react to what others say and think. Belief is not a package of truths that we take over from someone else but rather a trusting way of life that we must make our own. This means that belief concerns something personal — personal opinion, personal experiences, and forms of expression that touch us. In our pluralistic culture belief has become more individual. It is no longer self-evident (not only for Christianity but also for other religious groups) that people will follow their parents' belief system. Even though faith communities are available that define themselves clearly and in contrast with others, the transference of belief occurs less often than before within established organizations.

In the meantime we all face the question of what we are to believe, and this is not an easy question to answer. Some say that all belief boils down to the same thing; in that case the question does not need to be raised because what one believes is no longer of any real consequence. Others hold particular convictions to be true but do not feel that belief may be subjected to critical reflection. For them as well, the question does not need to be raised, for they know the answer: their belief is true and that of others is false. Still others find all belief nonsense; what do the differences between religions demonstrate other than the fact that people do not know what they are talking about and that it is impossible to have a rational discussion on religion?

These three positions hold basically that it is invalid to inquire into the *truth* of a belief. This is a remarkable point of view. From a personal perspective, it is odd to hold to a belief that cannot be justified. Proving belief is something different — it is impossible. Yet one expects that a person who believes will have reasons for doing so. Even if that belief has been learned from his or her parents, as is the case with many people, he or she must still have reasons for appropriating that belief. Not all are required to give a complete account for their belief, yet it is not unreasonable to expect someone to be able to give some reasons for holding a belief. One cannot justifiably say, "I believe what I believe but I cannot tell you why," any more than someone can say to his or her spouse, "I love you but I really do not know why," without marring the relationship. Believing implies insight as well. Although one can only partially describe such insight, one can say enough about it to explain it and justify it, at least partly, to someone else.

To avoid the question of the truth of a belief or to decide it in advance is also unacceptable from a societal point of view. Philosophical and religious traditions can have an enormous influence on the lives of believers. If humanists invite people to engage in self-development, could one then not expect them to be able to account for the social consequences of that development? If someone believes that people undergo several lives and that in their current existence they develop in a manner that conforms with the whole of their past lives, may one not ask what consequences this has for society? If people say that they must obey God above all else and that God wills the death of the godless, are those who disagree with this belief required to remain silent and to await patiently the consequences of this belief? Again, if a woman believes that the kingdom of God must be established on earth, is she not accountable to her neighbors who are affected by her behavior? Any civilization needs some amount of unity and consensus on norms and values. Philosophy and religion transmit ideals and norms, and that is why it is important for a society that its members understand one another with regard to their norms and values. Interreligious dialogue is of great importance to society.

Finally, it is unacceptable to continue to avoid the question of truth regarding religion and worldviews. This question belongs in intellectual discourse, and such discourse cannot ignore it. It would be absurd to examine everything, to question everything, and yet have nothing to say on religion. In universities people study solar systems and black holes, how nervous systems work, and how people react to commercial advertising. Scholars interpret literary texts and the positions of past religious philosophers in detail. Yet the question of whether what they say is true does not arise. People discuss karma and reincarnation, good and evil, question whether there is life after death, whether life has a purpose. Are we to believe that these questions do not deserve closer examination? People hold to particular beliefs for particular reasons, and these reasons can be justified, clarified, analyzed, and weighed against one another.

However one looks at it, the truth of belief is subject to discussion, and there will be no quick end to this discussion, for such a discussion does not proceed smoothly. We will see that different beliefs entail different views of reality and different worlds of experience with other ideals and values. People look at one another differently, and this is why comparing religions is not an easy matter. Religion concerns that which is decisive in life — matters that are of great value as well as those that are difficult to determine. For the most part arguments concerning belief consist in weighing arguments for the different views: the one argument supports this, the other that. Much can be said with respect to the possibility of natural theology, apologetics, or whatever one wishes to call the foundation of belief. It is not my desire, however, to duplicate or to summarize that discussion here. Rather, in this book I give an example of a justification of Christian belief, in view of which I weigh the conceptions of one tradition against those of another; and I summarize the advantages and disadvantages of each tradition. I indicate the weak points and dangers as I see them, while at the same time giving my own reflections and assessments. Readers should be responsible enough to de-

3

cide the issues for themselves. I do not ask what these assessments yield until the end of the book. The advantage of this approach is that I will have something concrete to fall back on: the argument that will have been made throughout the various chapters.

One reason for books such as this being relatively scarce lies in the great amount of material to cover. There are so many religious views; who can describe them all, do them justice, and be aware of all the relevant factors? It is virtually impossible. However, the maxim that the best is the enemy of the good applies here as well. Those who wish to cover everything and arrive at a comprehensive, watertight assessment will never be finished. But if one takes practical restrictions into account, attempts to reason carefully, and is aware of one's limitations, then it is still possible to reach some conclusions. The first restriction is to deal only with religious philosophies; nonreligious philosophies, such as socialism, Confucianism, and humanism, are excluded. In addition I limit myself to four of the major world religions: Buddhism, Hinduism, Christianity, and Islam, and then to particular schools within these religions. I refrain from discussing the New Age movement because, in the first place, rather than constituting one single school of thought, it encompasses a wide variety of beliefs and movements in which (from the Christian point of view) alternatives to or new interpretations of Christianity are sought. Second, the main themes of the New Age movement — related to nature, holism, karma, and reincarnation — are discussed in chapters two and three.[1]

The motifs that I will mention have not simply been plucked out of thin air. It is absurd to think that someone can assess religions impartially from an ivory tower and thus arrive at the one true religion. It is possible, however, for one to formulate one's own considerations. My starting point is then my own position; I describe other views as honestly and fairly as possible, ask questions, and in addition furnish considerations. In turn, I show the kind of questions others have had about our tradition. In this way I arrive at a dialogical account of Christian belief as I see it on the basis of study and discussion. No

1. For a discussion of and reflections on the New Age movement from the perspective of Christianity, see R. Kranenborg, ed., *New Age: Visies vanuit het christelijk geloof* (Amersfoort: De Horstink, 1993). For an explanation of experiences that support Christian belief and a reply to objections against it, see my *Waarom geloof? Argumenten voor en tegen geloof* (Kampen: Kok, 1985).

one can take everything into account, but that does not give one the right to neglect giving proper account of one's belief.

This is therefore an example of *critical dialogue*. Dialogue does not involve an exchange of ideas while avoiding critical questions. Rather, dialogue concerns truth and includes analyses, questions, answers, objections, judgments. A critical dialogue consists of four things: (1) examination of that which others actually believe; (2) articulation of one's own belief; (3) readiness to learn from one another: this concerns those aspects of the critique that are true and continue to obtain; (4) open discussion on mutual criticism with respect to the conceptions and practices of belief. A discussion that lacks the first element is not a dialogue but a monologue by someone who is not listening. An encounter without articulating and witnessing to one's own belief is a study project rather than a dialogue. A dialogue without willingness to learn from one another is a free exchange of thoughts. Readiness to learn from one another is needed in a discussion in which each party is taken seriously by the other parties. And there is every reason to take one another seriously, for traditions of belief that have guided the lives of people for more than a thousand years and in which many claim to have found well-being and peace evidently have something to say regarding the issue of what it is to be human.

An encounter without critical questions is no more than an initial acquaintance, where people do not want to get too close to one another. Many works from the first phases of dialogues and reports on conferences since the 1960s are permeated with this spirit of caution, and yet they have served to open the way for actual discussion. Still, the real encounter of the major traditions has yet to begin as far as traditionally Christian countries are concerned. Were other beliefs not regarded as underdeveloped for a number of decades? But now that the dialogue has become a worldwide necessity, it is time to ask those troublesome questions that cannot be ignored in considering the pros and cons of the major religions. Therefore, critical dialogue is a written contribution to the process in which people of many traditions meet and enter into discussions on what is ultimately true and good and of value to life. Before turning to that, however, I would like to make three further comments on dialogue.

First, who would dare to comment on the relation among Buddhism, Hinduism, Islam, and Christianity? In speaking too easily about Christianity or Hinduism, one quickly falls into generalities. Is belief not a very personal conviction? Should one not ask each person what he or she believes? This is indeed an aspect of religion; everyone forms his or her own view. But each religious tradition conveys a specific view and experience of reality that people can appropriate. All do this in their own way; some do much with it, while others do little. We realize only a few of the possibilities offered us by the tradition. The tradition is in itself important in that specific views and practices are inextricably bound up with a religious tradition; if these views and practices are abandoned, the religion changes fundamentally. True, traditions leave room for personal and contextual interpretation, but at the same time they do set boundaries. This enables us to comment on the one tradition from within the other tradition. This must occur in a dialogical attitude: the other is able to correct us and demonstrate that things are not as we thought them to be. The first requirement of dialogue is that the other be able to recognize him- or herself in the description that is offered.[2]

Second, dialogue looks at a religion from the perspective of its actual intentions. If I present as Christian something that others claim to be a watered-down or poor interpretation of Christian belief, then I am a poor discussion partner for a Buddhist, a humanist, or a Muslim. The norm for dialogue is not that which each person makes of it individually but that with which a religion or school is actually concerned. For that matter, the actual concern of a religion or school is not something that is fixed once and for all, since every religion is continually changing. This is why one is unable to establish "the truth" absolutely and why dialogue — as can be expected — requires discussion. Through discussion one can come to a better understanding of other traditions as well as one's own and sometimes arrive at a somewhat new interpretation of them as well.

Third, dialogue involves meeting and discussion. If one is to understand another tradition, then one will have to ensure that it is not misrepresented. To be sure, it is impossible to represent another religious tradition inside and out, but it is possible to give an interpretation that is as fair and sympathetic as possible, and to open oneself to criticism by the other. In this way one can learn from others. Rough contrasts are therefore to be avoided. It seems that a fruitful approach

---

2. This obtains, even though one cannot expect that someone in one's own tradition will describe one's belief exactly as one would describe it oneself.

would be to investigate how belief forms one's experience in particular, and for this reason I look closely at the way in which belief is worked out in someone's experience of reality.

As I see it, the reflections in this book are a kind of transitional work. After I had written exhaustively on the question of truth as an issue in and among religions in a much broader book,[3] the question remained as to how my belief related to that of others with respect to content. This book thus involves taking a position. Because others have the opportunity to react to what I am saying here and, as far as I am concerned, the last word has not been said, this book constitutes a step along the way.

The order of this book is as follows. In chapter two, "No-Self, Emptiness, and God," I examine a religious tradition that does not believe in God as the source of all things — Buddhism, a tradition that has also attracted followers in the West. I outline a number of Zen Buddhist ideas that merit attention and then suggest a few reasons for believing in God despite these ideas.

Chapter three, "God Has Many Names," concerns Hinduism. There are religions that regard the supreme as an inexhaustible source of everything that exists. For this reason the supreme can be revered in many ways and be called by many names. This is a belief encountered in many Hindus. What does this entail for belief in God and for the portrayal of humankind? Questions regarding reincarnation, karma, and caste cannot be ignored.

In chapter four, "The One God, the Prophet, and the Cross," I examine Islam. With regard to the number of adherents, Islam is the second largest religion that I discuss here. Muslims, Jews, and Christians confess one God. But is it the same God that they worship? How is God viewed? The Koran is central to Islam, and the Prophet plays a significant role in this religion. I consider the relation of the Koran and the Prophet to Christ on the one hand and to the Bible on the other.

Finally, in chapter five, ". . . No Other Gods. . . ," I discuss a number of general issues. These issues concern an explanation of the method of this book, the stance taken, and the question of the nature and value of critical dialogue. In addition, I discuss the relation between Christian and other beliefs in general. Do people believe in

3. See my *Religions and the Truth: Philosophical Reflections and Perspectives,* tr. J. W. Rebel (Grand Rapids: Eerdmans; Amsterdam: Rodopi, 1989).

other gods? If other beliefs are not seen as idolatry, how do we understand the commandment: "You shall have no other gods before me"? I thought it best to discuss the general questions at the end of the book by way of further clarification and conclusion. Discussing these questions at the beginning would make them quite broad and theoretical. The judgments in the previous chapters are the background against which I draw the conclusions. The general questions do come up indirectly, and occasionally explicitly, in the previous chapters. In the final chapter I draw together the main lines of the discussion and justify them in more detail.

2

No-Self, Emptiness, and God

2.1 Introduction

I will discuss Buddhist thought without attempting to give a survey of Buddhist "doctrine."[1] In what follows I outline a few points where Buddhism and Christianity converge, and also a few points where they diverge. The first topic is the idea of "no-self," which plays a great role in both religious traditions. I also consider the relationship between emptiness *(shunyata)* and belief in God, and the relation of belief to (so-called ordinary) life in this world. Both Christianity and Buddhism contain several different schools of thought, and with respect to the latter I will concentrate, although not exclusively, on the Zen philosophers of Kyoto — the Kyoto School. Zen Buddhism has preserved and continually renewed essential elements of classic Buddhist doctrine and practice, and with respect to dialogue it is good to begin with a tradition that does justice to the intentions of classical Buddhism.[2] As for Christianity, I will consider it from the viewpoint of my own, Protestant, tradition within the broader ecumenical movement.

I begin with Buddhism's strong points. Characteristic of Buddhist thought is its orientation toward changing one's mentality. Everything revolves around the person and her or his experiences. Buddhists speak of "humanity" and "the world" but do so from the

1. See my *Religions and the Truth: Philosophical Reflections and Perspectives,* tr. J. W. Rebel (Grand Rapids: Eerdmans; Amsterdam: Rodopi, 1989), ch. 4, and the literature cited there.

2. H. Bechert, "From Theravāda to Pure Land: Forms of Buddhist Thought and Life: Buddhist Perspectives," in H. Küng et al., *Christianity and the World Religions,* tr. P. Heinegg (Garden City, N.Y.: Doubleday, 1986), p. 373; see also his "Buddhism and Society: Buddhism in Our Time: Buddhist Perspectives," in ibid., p. 420.

perspective of personal experience. Only if one seeks to answer the question "What is humankind?" with reference to oneself is it possible to understand Buddhist treatments of this topic. The answer to such a question does not concern dry arguments and detached theories but personal insight into the truth. One can only be impressed by Buddhists' emphasis on compassion and pity, their respect for everything that lives, and their conscious experience of the world from moment to moment. Their perception of the connections in which one event evokes another and the accompanying relativization of the individual's place and self-interest also command respect. Buddhists seek clarity regarding the causes of all that occurs. Pivotal to their concern, expressed primarily in the central place that meditation has received, is the way in which people experience what happens to them. There is a friendly yet definite desire to help people solve their problems. The contemplative, spiritual path, as it is called, is fundamental.[3]

These characteristic emphases of Zen Buddhism are important for Western Christianity. Buddhism provides answers to problems that the churches have neglected for a long time. Since the antithesis between church and "the world" in Western culture has for the most part disappeared and "the world" is no longer regarded as evil and deceptive, a large part of the church has become secularized: the lifestyle of Christians does not differ all that much from that of other respectable people, and neither does their experience of reality. Christians do feel troubled about poverty and injustice but, generally speaking, are quite at home in this world, even though, particularly within the ecumenical movement, there are strong objections to the capitalist economy and the pollution of the environment. The Buddhist philosophers of the Kyoto School are also critical of industrial society. The Zen Buddhist philosopher Keiji Nishitani states, quite candidly, that in industrial societies, people tend to be governed by the pursuit of their desires — that is, by greed.[4] The purpose of meditation is to break through this greed and to

3. H. F. de Wit, *Contemplative Psychology,* tr. M. L. Baird (Pittsburgh: Duquesne University Press, 1991), pp. 149, 152ff.; cf. also idem, "The Contemplative Contribution to Interreligious Dialogue," in *Studies in Interreligious Dialogue* (henceforth *SID*) 1 (1991): 148ff., where the terms "way, path, spiritual development" and the phrase "traveling on the contemplative path" are used.

4. K. Nishitani, *Religion and Nothingness,* tr. J. Van Bragt (Berkeley: University of California Press, 1982), pp. 86-88. Cf. my "Aan het nihilisme voorbij: de godsdienstfilosofie van Nishitani," *Nederlands Theologisch Tijdschrift* 40 (1986): 143-59.

evoke a different perspective on existence. This attention to and training in changing one's mentality is one of Buddhism's strong points. One trains oneself in the true observation of what occurs. In haiku, a Japanese form of poetry, this true observation is articulated in an illustrative way, as can be seen from the following examples.

> Drenched through with droplets
> in morning rain the singing
> of the nightingales.[5]

> The nightingale came,
> and on the green field of moss
> it stood in silence.[6]

> Moonlight at evening,
> a snail, too, almost naked
> outside its house.[7]

> City people drive
> to their homes and in their hands
> red autumn leaves.[8]

In Buddhist schools of thought what is at issue is a new, different perspective in which the world of the moment is discovered at the moment that it occurs. This demands a receptive attitude, requiring an inversion or reversal of human consciousness. What occurs in the Buddhist view of reality is a turnabout from apparently ordinary experience to a more accurate perception. This reversal, the new perspective from which reality is seen altogether differently, becomes apparent in the following haiku:

---

5. Issa (1763-1827), in *Haiku: een jonge maan*, tr. J. van Tooren (Amsterdam: Meulenhoff, 1973), p. 119. Translators' note: Existing English translations for most of these Japanese poems were unavailable to me. I have supplied my own translations based on the Dutch translations given in the original Dutch edition of this book. I have used English translations where available and have indicated them in the notes.
6. Taigi (1709-1772), in *Haiku*, p. 119.
7. Issa, in *Haiku*, p. 185.
8. Meisetzu (1847-1926), in *Haiku*, p. 205.

Leading me along,
my shadow walked before me;
falls back in the moonlight.[9]

Who leads whom? Does a person lead the shadow or does the shadow lead the person? Who am "I" — I myself or my shadow? Which has primacy in a world where each — the one walking, the shadow, and the moon — exists in relation to the other two?

One can see a similar change of perspective in a haiku written by Basho shortly before he died on one of his journeys:

Traveling, I fell sick;
over the withered moorlands
my dream kept rambling.[10]

Living, traveling, or the wandering of the spirit in a dream — what distinguishes them from another? Is the writer's consciousness in life truly different from his consciousness in the dream? How can any distinction be made between them? The haiku thus evokes another perspective on reality, a perspective that is still and attentive to what occurs — not actively, but through meditation and contemplation.

The Christian church can learn a great deal from the Buddhist attention to personal formation and deepening. Modern culture offers many opportunities for distraction. For instance, the number of different films available is overwhelming. From another point of view, however, our culture is homogeneous: most people live lives similar to one another, buying and using the same sorts of things (the one more than the other). Many of the films broadcast on television deal, in fact, with only a few themes: violence, crime, and sex. From this point of view, therefore, culture is uniform and often superficial. For religion one must draw on deeper levels of existence, and meditation attempts to achieve this process of deepening and reversal. Because of the emphasis that many Buddhist schools place on the antithesis between the right and the wrong experience of the world, this is more than simply cheap salvation — it is a different and tranquil experience of reality.

9. Sodo (1641-1716), in *Haiku,* p. 231.
10. Basho (1644-1694), in *Haiku,* p. 261.

Buddhism and Christianity have some common ground, and it would appear that both traditions overlap on a number of points. I will discuss a few of these points, and, in doing so, will encounter a number of questions.

2.2 No-Self: Emptiness or a Renewed Person?

Buddhists and Christians agree that a great many problems stem from greed. People desire many things: to own beautiful things, to eat a varied diet of good food, to take interesting trips. Many of these things are to be appreciated: what, after all, is wrong with visiting a museum, owning a fine painting, or listening to good music on a compact disc? Whoever enjoys life appreciates such things. Yet becoming accustomed to pleasures brings sadness and disappointment, for the objects of desire often lie beyond the possibility of attainment or experience. Desire inevitably leads to disappointment. Moreover, desire acquires a hold on us, takes root in our hearts, becomes the center of our existence — an attitude that determines how we live. This obtains for everyone, regardless of differences among people and their circumstances. With regard to this fundamental characteristic of existence, differences are merely relative. Thus respectable people may have respectable desires and bad people bad desires, but deep down everyone is the same: the self is determined by desires.[11] The human "ego" is actually a collection of desires that defines the self-image. The entire "self" of which we are aware is actually composed of ideas about ourselves: we think "I still have to do this"; "if I do that, it will be okay"; or "if only that doesn't happen." Thus our "ego" consists of the ideals, images, and ideas about the reality of the life that we — partly consciously, partly unconsciously — have constructed around our "self" over the course of our lives.

Something is often wrong with these ideals, self-images, and

---

11. According to Romans 5, the essence of sin does not lie in doing wrong but in who one is. W. Schmithals, *Die theologische Anthropologie des Paulus* (Stuttgart: Kohlhammer, 1980), p. 41, writes that sin is not primarily a moral but an ontological category. Cf. p. 45: the law has caused sin to increase (even though or, more precisely, because the sinner *wants* to observe the law — cf. Rom. 5:18b-20).

assessments of reality. On the one hand, some people think too little of themselves; their ideals are so high that they cannot meet them and as a result have a poor self-image, frequently suffering pangs of conscience. On the other hand, there are those who think highly of themselves and often feel they are entitled to more than others. But things can go wrong here as well. Although not all people consult a psychologist or psychiatrist, almost everyone encounters one problem or another: adolescents often feel at a loss as to what to do; someone loses a job and is unable to find another; people undergo midlife crises and those approaching retirement age often experience great pain. I could go on. These problems stem from within ourselves, in the way we experience life, and both Buddhists and Christians agree that the central issue concerns the attitude we take in life.

The affinity between Buddhism and Christianity can be taken one step further. Both traditions believe that we must rise above being concerned with ourselves. Jesus himself said: "Do not worry about your life, what you will eat; or about your body, what you will wear. Life is more than food, and the body more than clothes. Consider the ravens: They do not sow or reap, they have no storeroom or barn; yet God feeds them. And how much more valuable you are than birds! Who of you by worrying can add a single hour to his life? Since you cannot do this very little thing, why do you worry about the rest?"[12] According to the Sermon on the Mount, one can be free of the cares of life, but only if one is also free from one's desires. This is stated repeatedly in the Gospels: "he who saves his life will lose it." One can let life go, be free of care, and wait to see what the next day brings. In other words, the "self" must be emptied if one is to find true life. This is the core of the gospel. Whoever believes is "in Christ" and finds life, the living water, the bread of life, and light.[13] True life is not what we usually think it to be, and we cannot attain it by our own effort: we must empty ourselves in order to be filled with the truth. This is clearly the case when Paul writes: "I have been crucified with Christ and I no longer live, but Christ lives in me."[14] This is only possible if Paul has given up his "ego" in order to make room for the

12. Luke 12:22-26. Cf. Matt 6:25-34. All quotations from the Bible are taken from the New International Version.
13. John 6:35; 7:38; 8:12; 14:6.
14. Gal. 2:20.

14

good: not his ego, but Christ. It is this that is often viewed as the heart of the gospel, particularly in more mystic and pietistic Christian circles. "Being in Christ" is the core of faith: surrendering ourselves in faith to God so as to be guided entirely by Christ, and making our own desires and wishes subservient to God's will.

Buddhism also speaks of emptying the ego. The root of desire and attachment lies in cherishing the "self." But if we are honest we know that our "selves" are only a collection of the ideals and desires that we have built up in the past. However, these ideals and norms that constitute the "self" are what cause people to stand in the way of themselves. Life usually follows a course different from our ideals, resulting in difficulties because we desire something other than what life offers. We must learn to allow ourselves to be carried along in such a way that we remain open to seeing what the best course is in every new situation. We must not become attached to ideals and certainly not to possessions: whoever does so will inevitably suffer when reality overtakes him or her. Buddhists and Christians say that we must learn to let go. We must empty ourselves of the self and realize the no-self. Buddhists teach emptiness *(shunyata):* the "ego," as it were, is *dissolved.* When there is no longer an "ego" that wants to control and to satisfy desires, then we can accept whatever happens. Many of the causes of suffering and worry are thus avoided. As Ikkyu, an ancient Buddhist poet, says:

> If I do not decide
> The dwelling place
> Of my future,
> How is it possible
> That I should lose my way?[15]

I am like a leaf in the wind, and who knows where the wind goes? I see where I am going; I live every moment consciously, yet without attachment or desire. I will not be disappointed, because my desires are extinguished. I cannot become lost, for I have no goal. I am a leaf in the wind, taken up into the large whole, determined by a web of factors. If

15. Ikkyu (d. 1481), in *The Buddha Eye: An Anthology of the Kyoto School,* ed. F. Franck (New York: Crossroad, 1982), p. 80.

I am truly empty, there is no "self," no personal, independent identity, but only consciousness from moment to moment. I therefore no longer need to fear the danger of becoming lost or death itself:

> Our real mind
> Has no beginning,
> No end;
> Do not fancy
> That we are born, and die.[16]

The Buddhist answer to the pain that death brings — the parting, the fear, the uncertainty about what comes after death — is that "I" do not exist as a separate individual. I exist — but without beginning and without end. I am only a moment in the great series of events of which I am a part. Birth and death, like powder in water, are dissolved. *Enlightenment,* the goal of meditation, is learning to see ourselves as such — a moment in the continuous stream of events which determines us and of which each of us is a part.

Christianity and Buddhism overlap with regard to the emptiness of the no-self *(anatman)*. Yet, given the further context of each faith, there are also fundamental differences. The emptiness of the no-self in Christian belief is "filled" with "Christ" and is a new "self" that is guided by Christ, rather than a no-self. Paul's words "I no longer live, but Christ" are intended to banish every thought of merit. The believer who, according to the Johannine expression, "is in Christ," is a new person, born again, as it were.[17] Paul's no-self is a new self: "Therefore, if anyone is in Christ, he is a new creation; the old has gone, the new has come!"[18] A new nonegotistical self exists, having both individuality and a name that is written in the palm of God's hand, as it is often said. In Christian belief the negation of the egotis-

---

16. Ibid.

17. John 3:3. Cf. R. Bultmann, *Gospel of John,* tr. and ed. G. R. Beasley-Murray et al. (Philadelphia: Westminster, 1971), p. 137: "Rebirth means . . . something more than an improvement in man; it means man receives a new *origin,* and this is manifestly something he cannot give to himself," with reference to Calvin ("non partis unius correctionem, sed renovationem totius naturae").

18. 2 Cor. 5:17. Cf. Schmithals, *Die theologische Anthropologie des Paulus,* p. 41, on people as "relational beings" *(Beziehungswesen),* fundamentally determined either by their existence *coram Deo* or by living *coram se ipso* (Rom. 14:6ff.).

tical ego does not imply no-self but rather, conversely, the confirmation of the person. The freedom from care in the Sermon of the
Mount is based on the fact that people are more important than birds,
whom "the Father" supplies with all that they need. The fact that
death is no longer to be feared does not arise because "I" am not "I"
but because, in Christ, life has triumphed over death. Death is not
dissolved here but conquered. It is not because a person has no "ego"
and no goal that she or he does not become lost, but because, no
matter what happens, she or he will return home.

We thus come to the question of *anatman* (no-self) in the Buddhist teaching. If it is the wrong self that is defeated, is there not a
real "ego," someone with a name who is addressed by that name,
someone who exists in relation to others and thus has (or "is") a
separate individuality? Can we speak properly of the human personality if we say no more than that the person is *anatman* (no-soul, no-self)?
Nishitani states that the person in the state of enlightenment enters
into a new way of being human: "the self, in being the self, is not the
self." But what is the status of this new, good self?[19] Is the new
enlightened person not still an active being with individual responsibility and her or his own place in the community?

Actions, however, lie on a different level than emptiness. Although the enlightened person does exist in a social and historical
context, he is essentially determined by the religious dimension of
existence. This religious dimension does not belong to spatiotemporal
existence, which is the process of life and death. Life and death are
inseparable; the historical existence of the person is instituted by
living-dying and birth-death. Concrete life is enacted in the endless
changes of life and the many relations in which people exist. As a piece
of wood drifts on the sea and is driven by the wind and waves, so a
person drifts among the many powers that act on him or her: physical
regularities, climatic changes, laws and coincidences of economic life,
the psychological circumstances that influence one's state of mind —
in short, the context of a person's life. People are elements in the great
process *(samsara)* of which they are a part. The religious dimension,
however, is separate from this: it falls outside this process and outside
time. Salvation is realized here and now, and refers to another dimen-

19. Nishitani, *Religion and Nothingness,* p. 277; cf. pp. 27, 35; see my *Religions
and the Truth,* pp. 176-80.

17

sion of life, a dimension of an order completely different from this temporal existence: "eternity in the midst of time."[20] Zen is not concerned with salvation in the future, but with the emptiness and detachment of now.

Social obligations and morality fall within samsara, the social and biological life of humans, and thus do not apply at the level of religion and salvation. Good and evil are categories of everyday life and as such are determined by many influences. They are interwoven with life: our insight into them is limited, and absolute — therefore true — judgments about them are impossible. We are caught in the relations within which we live; all our judgments are culturally determined. The prejudices of our time restrict us; our egos and false desires determine who we are. Good and evil are categories belonging to this world in which the one determines the other; they are interdependent and offer no absolute guide for action.[21] It can be seen how bound we are to evil when we try to do good. The very distinction between good and evil rests on the fact that one is bound by the latter. Masao Abe, the Zen master and philosopher, writes very personally about this: "My personal experience was such that, the more I tried to do good and avoid evil, the more I realized that I was far removed from good and bound by evil. My moral life resulted in the realization of the radical evil at the bottom of the fight between good and evil and my fundamental ignorance of the ultimate truth."[22]

If we cannot transcend the difference between good and evil, then we are still bound by radical evil. Because good and evil are interwoven with life, we must transcend the ordinary life of birth and death, good and evil. But that which we must let go is life itself; there is no other life than this life. We cannot make this life any better. We do not recognize any true values, we have no real "ego," and it is precisely in the belief that we are somebody, that we have a "self," and even recognize the difference between good and evil, that the mechanism of attachment and sorrow lies. It is a classic Buddhist idea that doing that which is recognized as good or as evil is important with respect to reincarnation, be it at a higher or a lower

20. Masao Abe, "A Rejoinder," in *The Emptying God: A Buddhist-Jewish-Christian Conversation,* ed. J. B. Cobb and C. Ives (Maryknoll, N.Y.: Orbis, 1990), pp. 190-91.
21. Abe, *Zen and Western Thought* (Houndmills: Macmillan, 1985), pp. 190, 191.
22. Abe, "Rejoinder," p. 188.

level. But as far as ultimate redemption is concerned, good works are not important.

At a deeper level, both good and bad deeds are *only deeds,* since they are motivated by attachment to oneself and to life. Because of this they prolong the existence characterized by samsara.[23] Abe writes that for him it entailed the death of his ego when he realized that radical evil lay at the foundation of the struggle for good. This is called the *great death,* as opposed to the small, the "ordinary," death. The great victory is not immortality but rather victory over the self, the great death. This great death points us to the foundation of life, which itself lies outside samsara: eternity, the now, emptiness, fullness, transcendence — it cannot be expressed in words, because (in a sense) it lies outside samsara. In order to indicate that life has changed, one speaks of life-or-death or death-or-life.[24] The old self has died and something new has taken its place. But what? Nothing other than what was already there: the same thing but now different; a self that is no-self. But this self is now a person who is no longer defined by attachment and ignorance, and is therefore characterized by *complete receptivity.* If one has died the great death, become impartial, and is no longer blind, then one is able to see and accept things as they are. One has nothing more to fear; one can face everything and one has dismantled all internal defense mechanisms. One lives in reality as it is — continually changing and new each moment. Every new configuration of facts can be faced and everything can be experienced in its own uniqueness. One no longer needs to speculate about a being behind things, but rather sees them exactly as they appear in the many relations in which they exist. *Shunyata* is unlimited openness. In this way an attitude of pure spontaneity and naturalness *(jinen)* arises.[25]

Zen Buddhism thus involves an ethics of virtue; every moralist who cannot view things from the perspective of *shunyata,* and cannot feel naturally, is caught in the web of attachment and karma, so that she or he cannot conquer radical evil (without first dying the great death). This naturalness consists primarily of virtuous wisdom *(prajna)* and compassion *(karuna).* Wisdom is seeing and understanding that

23. Abe, "Kenotic God and Dynamic Sunyata," in *Emptying God,* p. 41; the question of good and evil is also discussed in the following paragraphs.

24. For example, Nishitani, *Religion and Nothingness,* pp. 93-94.

25. Abe, "Kenotic God and Dynamic Sunyata," pp. 30ff.

which is observed in the relations within which the observed really exists. Compassion means that we are moved by pity to help our fellow beings abandon attachment and blindness. Because this is done naturally and spontaneously, it transcends morality.[26] Religion provides the basis for detached (moral) judgments without confronting one with the dilemma of having to choose between good and evil. It therefore offers a fixed point within and outside a reality that is causally determined so that one is free of radical evil, thus allowing the possibility of right action.[27] On the religious level, things are exactly as they appear and no more: mountains are mountains, rivers are rivers, an earthquake is an earthquake, and sunshine is sunshine. In this superhuman dimension all these phenomena appear in their suchness, that is, as they are, neither good nor bad.[28]

Shunyata is openness to phenomena. It is a dynamic attitude, not an extraordinary state in which one is withdrawn from the world, but a dynamic openness in which one spontaneously acts wisely and compassionately.

Here is a fundamental difference with respect to Christianity. Christian faith does not elevate one above good and evil but involves the forgiveness of one's sins. One is asked to repent and to live according to the demands of the kingdom of God rather than those of "this world," that is, the prevalent way of life. The ideals toward which one must strive are justice and peace; moderation and patience are prominent virtues. A person turns to God not in self-exaltation but in humility, and to one's neighbor in solidarity. Christianity also offers a different perspective on reality and a fixed point beyond existence in this world. Repentance and conversion are even equated with death. Whereas Zen philosophers speak of the great death, the apostle Paul says that whoever is baptized is buried with Christ

26. Ibid., p. 32: "Such transmoral compassionate activities and universal salvation are possible because they come spontaneously out of the unfathomable depth of Sunyata and because they are based on the great affirmation of all things realized through wisdom." Abe responds to Eugene B. Borowitz's comment in "Dynamic Sunyata and the God Whose Glory Fills the Universe," in *Emptying God,* p. 82, that the primary task of Judaism is to achieve holiness by living justly (and that religion and morality are therefore interwoven), with the comment that Judaism and Buddhism clearly differ. Cf. Abe, "Rejoinder," p. 185.

27. Abe, "Rejoinder," p. 182.

28. Abe, "Kenotic God and Dynamic Sunyata," p. 49.

"through baptism into death in order that, just as Christ was raised from the dead through the glory of the Father, we too may live a new life."[29] Death is the symbol of a person's deep religious renewal for Paul as well. It is the transition to everlasting life. Thus there is a parallel between the great death in Zen Buddhism and death in Christian faith, but there are also fundamental discrepancies. I discuss these more fully later, but I would like to mention two here: first, the affirmation of the human being as a person; second, the thesis of the reformers that a person is both a sinner and justified at the same time.

Baptism demonstrates that a person is accepted by God as he or she is. Grace is "free," that is, it is not given on the basis of any special merit of the person concerned but only on the basis of God's love. God allows me to be. A person — young or old — is baptized and given a name. This person's identity does not consist of a being in or behind the person — a point on which Christians and Buddhists agree — but in the name by which he or she is called. Buddhists teach that everything is related to everything (the doctrine of mutually dependent existence); enlightenment involves a person merging completely into the great interdependent whole. Within Zen Buddhism relationality is the relatedness of everything to everything else; within Christianity relationality involves humanity and the relation between God and people. One does not realize emptiness, but becomes a neighbor to other human beings. This is the first difference.

The second difference coheres closely with the first. Baptized Christians live in this world and not everything they do is good. In Reformational theology this is expressed by saying that the person is simultaneously a sinner and justified: *simul iustus et peccator.*[30] People are sinners and the concrete existence of a believer is certainly not perfect. There is no enlightenment; rather, sin, which can weigh heavily on a person, has not gone away. We are woven into a web of impotence, shortsightedness, and greed. At the same time, however, believers are justified through faith in God's grace — a "declarative," imputed righteousness. They do not achieve this righteousness them-

29. Rom. 6:4.
30. G. C. Berkouwer, *Faith and Sanctification,* tr. J. Vriend (Grand Rapids: Eerdmans, 1952), pp. 71-76, 110-13.

selves but receive it by the grace of God.[31] Believers are exempt from worry because God loves them and forgives their sin for Christ's sake, thus enabling them to devote themselves completely to the kingdom of God. In this way one can understand Paul's claim that "it is not 'I' but Christ in me" with reference to the good that he does. He would not make such a claim in reference to what he does wrong: what is good comes from God, but what is wrong is due to the old sinful person.[32] These two aspects are often in conflict with each other in people,[33] but this need not cause too much concern, for God does not hold the wrong against them. It is not by fulfilling the demands of the law but by the grace of God that one becomes good, and it is this that is the source of the Christian's freedom.[34] These are the two sides of the doctrine of *simul iustus et peccator:* fundamentally justified, yet still living in a broken world as a "child of God" who continually falls short of the mark.

One could ask an unlimited number of questions. Buddhists could ask how radical the renewal is if the believer is not only justified but also and simultaneously a sinner, retaining her or his own identity — even beyond death! Buddhists would feel that it should be even more radical. One must rid oneself of one's old identity so that the old self is gone: non-*peccator* and non-*iustus*. The dilemma of sinful/not sinful must be surmounted, and here grace can play a role. In Amida Buddhism one may call on the grace of the Amida Buddha, who may grant a person reincarnation in the Pure Land, where he or she can actually attain nirvana. Grace is decisive here. According to G. Hoshino, Amida Buddhism teaches that since people are not able to empty themselves, redemption can only occur on the basis of a power that comes from elsewhere. The difference between Amida Buddhism and Christianity is that the latter sees the gracious God as an "opposite," a "Person" who enters into a relationship with human beings, whereas Buddhism con-

---

31. Cf. G. C. Berkouwer, *Faith and Justification,* tr. L. B. Smedes (Grand Rapids: Eerdmans, 1954), pp. 90-91; cf. pp. 79ff.; H. Berkhof, *Christian Faith,* tr. S. Woudstra (Grand Rapids: Eerdmans, 1979), pp. 432-35, 443-45; H. Ridderbos, *Paul: An Outline of His Theology,* tr. J. R. De Witt (Grand Rapids: Eerdmans, 1975), particularly pp. 176-78.

32. Eph. 4:2; Col. 3:10.

33. Rom. 7:23.

34. Gal. 5:1-6, 13-24.

siders the absolute to be, at bottom, one with mundane reality.[35] Because relations among people play such a large role in Christianity, the personality of God and people is important[36] — God knows the name of each person. There is nothing wrong with the will to live, for it is a gift of God.[37] Christians could ask with respect to the Buddhist view (a) how Amida Buddha, the bestower of grace, can be essentially one with the receiver of grace; (b) how does the one who empties the self "realize" wisdom and become filled with compassion; and (3) what does this compassion mean in the experience of a world full of good and evil.[38] I return to this last question below.

2.3 A Force Field and "God"

I now take up the question of reality, which Buddhists experience as emptiness on the one hand and Christians as faith on the other. Buddhism views the reality of the world as completely determined. It is an aggregate of interactive powers, each of which is determined by the others. Nothing is permanent. Just as no person has a lasting ego, so there is nothing that has any permanence of its own. A table consists of four legs and a flat surface; if one leg breaks, it is no longer a table. Twilight is a play of light: transitory like a haiku, beautiful and evanescent. Pain comes and goes. We are accustomed to ascribing individual existence and permanence to things, but whoever realizes *shunyata* will not do so. Not only is the human ego empty but the world as a whole is empty as well. What are we to make of that?

35. G. Hoshino, "Das Verhältnis des buddhistischen Denkens zu Karl Barth," in *Antwort,* Festschrift K. Barth (Zürich: Zollikon, 1956), pp. 433, 429. Cf. Barth's view in *Church Dogmatics* I/2, ed. G. W. Bromiley and T. F. Torrance, tr. G. T. Thomson and H. Knight (Edinburgh: T. & T. Clark, 1956), pp. 340-44.

36. Cf. L. J. van den Brom, "Hoe 'eeuwig' is eeuwig leven?" in *Houdt het op met de dood?* ed. A. W. Musschenga and H. Vroom (Kampen: Kok, 1989), pp. 105-7, 111-13; and my "Wie zullen wij zijn? De verwachting van een eeuwig leven en de menselijke identiteit," in ibid., pp. 129-34.

37. J. B. Cobb, "On the Deepening of Buddhism," in *Emptying God,* p. 98.

38. Cf. John Cobb, *Beyond Dialogue* (Philadelphia: Fortress, 1982), pp. 136-40, on the affinities and differences between Christianity and Buddhism, particularly in relation to Pure Land Buddhism, in connection with the issue of what the basis for the expectation of grace is.

Nishitani gives an indication of what one experiences in this case: a field of force, or power.[39] One can conceive of this by looking, as it were, at things from a distance. From such a view, everything is determined; the one thing comes into being because of another. The raising of my hand is caused by something else, and that in turn is caused by yet something else. It also has an effect — someone waves back. Saying things that are ugly or nice also has causes and effects. Everything is linked together.

We are sometimes able to experience something of this. It is not anything like the enlightenment for which one strives in Buddhism, but it is an experience that gives some indication of what enlightenment is about. Sometimes one is able to experience oneself and the aggregate of things as a great coherent whole of which one is a part, yet without experiencing these things from within oneself as the center of one's own experience.[40] One then realizes where others are, how acquaintances feel, their expectations and disappointments; and events are experienced as a great stream of correlated causes and effects. As a result, the "self" is cancelled as an independent factor having its own role, and what remains is a "self" as an element alongside other elements in the great whole of things. This can be experienced in a moment, a transparent "now," of which the past and the future are dimensions. Rather than having a sense of being raised above things and looking down on them, one has a sense of standing in the midst of them and being part of them. The experience of enlightenment lies, I suppose, in prolonging this experience. Enlightenment must be a much more intense and inclusive experience than the one just described; it leads to a permanently altered experience of reality. One practices this experience through meditation — it cannot be forced, since the crux of such an experience is that one is no longer in possession of oneself but has been detached from oneself. Thus one learns to experience reality in two ways simultaneously: first, in the sense indicated as a field of power or as a great chain of cause and effect; second, as the ordinary reality in which one as a person lives

39. Nishitani, *Religion and Nothingness,* pp. 150-52, 166; cf. my "Aan het nihilisme voorbij," p. 151.

40. Similar experiences are described more than once by Anne Bancroft in *Weavers of Wisdom: Women Mystics of the Twentieth Century,* tr. W. M. J. Meissner-Stibbe (Arkana: Mirananda, 1989), for example, on pp. 18, 49, 99.

and acts.[41] In this way one experiences the complete whole of things: one is absorbed. Kitaro Nishida, another philosopher of the Kyoto School, writes that this is eternal love, eternal happiness, and eternal peace.[42]

Christian belief also involves an experience of mundane reality that differs from the "ordinary" experience. Every person has his or her own activities; usually one's individual life is central. But in faith one realizes that the whole world is God's creation, a different experience of reality that is evoked in the liturgy of Christian church services. At the beginning of the service the minister usually says: "Our help is in the name of the Lord, who made heaven and earth." With these words life is placed within one great coherent whole. Removed from momentary concerns, from individual fears and joys, the people are placed within the great whole of all things. In this Buddhism and Christianity agree.

The difference, however, is that the Christian faith does not see the world as an entity of factors that completely determine one another. Moreover, the world has value in itself (even though it has not entirely fulfilled God's intention for his "creation"):[43] it has a beginning and will have an end. The world has its origin in God, and although there is much wrong with it now, God does not, as the words at the beginning of the worship service state, let go of the work of his hands. The denial of the world's independence (in the words "who made heaven and earth") goes hand in hand with the confirmation of the world's value. Life is given a place; it is designated *coram Deo* (before the face of God). At the same time, a norm is given: God's intention for this world. God's grace and power will achieve a good end for his work, and for this reason believers can leave the concerns of their existence behind. God is not only the Exalted One, whose

41. "Samsara is nirvana," as it is often expressed. The conditioned existence of daily life (samsara) is identical to the life experienced in enlightenment (nirvana).

42. Kitaro Nishida, *An Inquiry into the Good,* tr. Masao Abe and C. Ives (New Haven and London: Yale University Press, 1990), p. 83.

43. "Creation," it has been argued, is not the same as "nature." In principle, nature is ambiguous because it includes elements that are conducive for human and animal existence (i.e., edible fruits) as well as destructive elements (i.e., poisonous fruits). In the story of Genesis, creation ("and God saw that it was good") precedes the Fall, after which the earth produces thorns and thistles (which are not good). Thus nature, as such, is not good.

being cannot be understood by anyone, but also the One Who Is Near, inspiring people through his Spirit, giving strength and support. Prayer allows Christians the opportunity to bring their concerns to God, to reflect on their life, and to direct it toward the real values of existence. In principle, therefore, just as with a person's individuality, Christianity gives a positive evaluation of living in the world. Although much in the world is wrong, much is also good, and people are responsible for preserving what is good and opposing what is wrong. People can enjoy what is good and beautiful, such as companionship, children at play, art, as well as much in nature itself. They should contribute to culture and preserve the good in nature. This is why dams are built to protect people against floods and why we should protect plants and animals if necessary.

Thus a Christian experience of reality goes hand in hand with a particular way of looking at the "ordinary" world. I have just described an experience of being included in the coherence of *all* things — the continuation of which entails enlightenment. From a biblical point of view the inclusive unity of all things becomes problematic: a central Buddhist insight is that all things originated in their mutual dependence ("dependent coorigination"), which is contrary to how a Christian experiences the world. It is true that Christian belief also involves the awareness of being an element in the whole of the world, but the world is experienced in the *brokenness of good and evil,* justice and injustice. Christian belief does not involve an experience of the totality of the world of nature, the All, or the causal coherence of all things of which people are individual parts. All things are not to be seen as a whole, but in their brokenness. The world and nature are incomplete, within which evil plays a significant and unique role. Sometimes evil is historical, in which case it is caused by people: the bad solution to one war is often the cause of the next. Buddhists are very much attuned to the evil consequences of wrong actions, but adherents of Judaism, Christianity, and Islam clearly distinguish good from evil and are never able to place the two within an inclusive relationship, as if good and evil are parts of a whole with equal status. For this reason as well, salvation does not entail the transcendence of good and evil, which would allow one to view them as relative. The salvation of the gospel is primarily God's gracious acceptance of people, forgiveness of sin, and the inspiration to do good. The contrast between good and evil is not relative. Abe often quotes a verse from the

Sermon on the Mount which states that God causes the sun to rise on the evil and the good and sends rain on the righteous and the unrighteous, for he loves not only those who love him but also those who hate him. This is the perfection of his love.[44] This does not, however, entail any relativization of the distinction between good and evil, as Abe holds, but it is a token of God's boundless love that in his mercy he even reaches out to those who hate him and harm the world order as he intended it.

Christianity has a different relativization of good and evil people. I have already mentioned it: those who live by the rules are not automatically better than thieves (though it is usually better from a societal point of view if most people adhere to the rules). In many cases people are better off if they do so; moreover, they may have better friends, less difficulties, and live under better circumstances. *Coram Deo,* however, goes beyond the question of whether one lives properly. Buddhism recognizes this relativization too, as we have already seen: by doing good deeds, the wheel of life still turns and one is not released from samsara. But according to Christianity, good and evil belong to the moral order of life. God, who is beyond all comprehension and lives in a light unapproachable and unfathomable to humans, reveals himself to people in this world. He does not transcend good and evil but has shown himself to be good.[45] God has revealed himself in earthly reality, made himself known in it, and demonstrates that he is a participant in a covenantal history between himself and people. This history involves *this* world, and the covenant contains rules and stipulations. The purpose of the covenant is that justice, peace, and faith will blossom like a rose, that each individual will have her or his fair share; that mothers and fathers will be able to feed and clothe their children, that young people will meet with care, love, compassion, and wisdom, the elderly will be able to live in security, and everyone in this world will have a home, shelter, and food — not excluding the concern for nature.

But the brokenness of this world involves pain and risk. Whoever

44. Matt. 5:45-46.

45. In my opinion, goodness must be regarded as an open and therefore not necessary property of God; see my "God and Goodness," in *Christian Faith and Philosophical Theology: Essays in Honour of Vincent Brümmer,* ed. G. van den Brink et al. (Kampen: Kok Pharos, 1992), pp. 240-57.

loves others cannot avoid pain and disappointment, because people are mortal and are seldom completely trustworthy. I will return in detail to the dark side of life, to misery and obstinacy. Here I simply want to make clear that the Bible is no stranger to misery (read the Psalms!) and that injustice and misery are not accepted; complaints are made again and again. In the biblical wisdom literature this resistance is combined with wisdom and skepticism, but justice, peace, and love are praised and viewed as the real intention of this life. Ecclesiastes says that there is a time to weep and a time to laugh, a time to plant and a time to uproot, but this does not lead to a call to combat evil by detaching oneself internally from the world.[46]

Christian faith is concerned with this world, and this is why hope for the future entails a new earth: improved yet earthly, changed yet still creation. A fault line runs through this world. To be sure, it is not always clear to us exactly where the boundary lies, but some things are good and others evil. For this reason as well, Christianity does not see the world as a closed chain of causal relations and "dependent coorigination."

Within Christian belief a monistic or holistic view of reality (which, as implied by these words, places *all* things in one all-embracing framework) is out of the question.[47] This can already be seen in the cross, the central symbol in Christianity. The cross is the symbol of the weakness that, through humiliation, conquers strength and of the good that triumphs over evil. The gospel's point of contact is not constituted primarily by the notion of the whole of reality but by the realities of injustice, failure, misery, sin, and wonder and awe. The distinction between death and life, between evil and good, is not relativized by the interrelationship of all things. The individual is not submerged in the whole, as it were, but rather confirmed in her or his own right.

A salvation that does not "raise" the person but confirms him or her is, according to Buddhists, only a half-salvation, for the value of the individual person remains. Everyone's name is used by others and is known by God. Buddhists feel that the realization of *shunyata*

---

46. Eccl. 3:2-8.
47. Cf. G. C. Berkouwer, *Sin,* tr. P. C. Holtrop (Grand Rapids: Eerdmans, 1971), pp. 62-66, 98. This is because of the confession "Deus non causa peccati" (God is not the cause of sin).

reaches further because the distinction between self and no-self is no longer valid — it is a state of not-being-distinguished, and this state cannot be expressed in words (because expressing something in words is to name it and thus distinguish it from something else). Whoever wishes to know what "emptiness" means must leave ordinary logic behind. It concerns an experiencing of things in an immense force field: everything that exists is part of this field in which forces act on one another. Nothing has its own identity; in other words, everything is void of anything permanent that would fall outside the force field. The whole of reality is part of this field in which things mutually influence one another. The realization of the emptiness of everything, including the self, is a sort of absorption into this whole, a total experience of relatedness with all things, allowing oneself to drift along the great stream and to dive in:

> If I do not decide
> The dwelling place
> Of my future,
> How is it possible
> That I should lose my way?

Fear is thus negated; one has nothing to lose.

Suffering is neutralized in this way as well. The Four Noble Truths of Buddhism explain the cause of suffering and how to eliminate it. Whoever realizes *shunyata* is no longer vulnerable to suffering: "in true Buddhist great compassion, one does not suffer even if one is in the midst of suffering, for through the death of the ego one has become identical with absolute *Mu* [= nothing]," writes Abe. To be sure, this does not mean that one is insensitive to suffering; indeed, through compassion one is able to "suffer with others," yet one remains undisturbed by it.[48] The evil in the world occurs in the realm of samsara, the determined existence in which good and evil, weal and woe occupy such a prominent place. This also obtains for the great disasters of world history. They are part of the whole in which one exists as well; to this extent one shares the responsibility for the great mistakes. In samsara everyone shares in evil. One must guard against absolutizing great evils, Abe writes, such as Auschwitz and

---

48. Abe, *Zen and Western Thought,* p. 183.

29

Hiroshima; the more one is emotionally involved with and determined by evil, the more evil determines future events. Conversely, one must realize that the Holocaust is also part of the web of human history; in order to render it harmless one must come to realize that even these events are relational (in the sense of related to all the rest) and nonsubstantial (in the sense of not having their own being or existence). Thus Abe calls the Holocaust a relative rather than an absolute evil.[49] And it can only be relative, for Abe places the whole of the distinction between good and evil, just and unjust, in the realm of relative reality, of samsara, that one transcends through the attitude of *shunyata.* In short, in the state of emancipation, mountains are mountains, the warmth of the morning sun on the bay is the warmth of the sun, the destruction of a city due to an earthquake is the destruction of a city, but it no longer causes pain, because one has become a spectator and no longer has an identity within samsara.

Within other traditions (theistic religions and several schools in Western philosophy), this view gives rise to the question as to what unifies the stream of things and what determines the "place where I live in my future." Nishida uses the word "god," but one must not think here of a creator who has made the world and even taken a stance against the world and plays a role in history. He writes that in a sense "god" is the cause of reality, the unity of the universe, of which all things are a part.[50] Strictly speaking, therefore, "god" is not a being in whom one can believe and trust, but a "god" that one is able to realize if one realizes the unity of all things in one's existence through "the great death" — thereby losing one's existence as self and finding the real being-such of existence.[51]

49. Abe, "Kenotic God and Dynamic Sunyata," p. 52; idem, "Rejoinder," p. 187, among others, in answer to criticism by Borowitz, "Dynamic Sunyata and the God Whose Glory Fills the Universe," in *Emptying God,* pp. 83-84; cf. Cobb, "On the Deepening of Buddhism," in ibid., p. 93. On the question of the relativity of hunger, the threat of war, sickness, etc., in a different context, cf. H. Waldenfels, *De Gekreuzigte und die Weltreligionen* (Zurich: Benziger, 1983), pp. 52-53; cf. p. 62.

50. Nishida, *Inquiry into the Good,* p. 82: "An immoral activity clearly functions at the base of the establishment of reality, and it is by means of this activity that reality is established"; and: "God is in these senses the unifier of the universe, the base of reality; and because God is no-thing, there is no place where God is not, and no place where God does not function."

51. H. Bechert, "The Historical Buddha: His Teaching as a Way to Redemp-

From the point of Christianity and Western metaphysics, the Buddhist view does not offer any explanation for the origin of the world. A Christian may ask: How is it that there is a world in which I can be submerged and of which I am part? Conversely, a Buddhist may bring up once more the old question of God's origin. The answer that God simply exists and that his existence is unfathomable to humans does not say much. The Buddhist may ask why God allows evil to exist, and the Christian may ask why people were ever wrong about the emptiness in all things.

Many Christians speak about God — the mystery of reality — *over against* the world ("I am God and not man — the Holy One among you"),[52] as one who sympathizes with the world ("for God so loved the world . . ."),[53] and not about the divine as the ground of all things that, as the unity of all things, coheres with all things. That Christians draw back from a depiction in which "god" permeates all things equally stems from the fear that if all things cohere equally with "god," then everything is equally holy or profane, and a prophetic approach and solidarity fade away.[54]

---

tion: Buddhist Perspectives," in Küng et al., *Christianity and the World Religions,* p. 304, says that Indonesian Buddhists, in connection with government policy regarding religion at the time that forced them to express themselves on belief in God, equated various terms with the concept of God: nirvana, Adibuddha (the primal Buddha), *shunyata,* or dharma. Bechert remarks that the quest for God is not an important theme for Buddhists.

52. Hos. 11:9.

53. John 3:16.

54. The same critique can be found in Cobb, "On the Deepening of Buddhism," in *Emptying God,* p. 99: "The focus is on what is always and everywhere the same." What has happened to the consideration of specific problems (p. 96)? I will forego a discussion of Abe's summary of divine kenosis: God is God, because he empties himself and is not God. Abe has grasped much of Christian belief and poses penetrating questions from which Christian theology can learn more than from discussion with uninformed atheists (cf. the remarks of Cobb and Moltmann in their contributions in *Emptying God*), but Abe's position also raises the objection that the *entire* world is the emptied God; I will also forego Abe's penetrating description of Jesus Christ. Cf. the various contributions in *Emptying God* and Masao Abe, "Kenosis and Emptiness," in *Buddhist Emptiness and Christian Trinity: Essays and Explorations,* ed. R. Corles and P. F. Knitter (New York: Paulist, 1990), pp. 5-25. Cf. the reaction of H. Küng, "God's Self-Renunciation and Buddhist Emptiness: A Christian Response to Masao Abe," in ibid., pp. 26-43; and Masao Abe, "God and Absolute Nothingness," *SID* 1 (1991): 58-69.

2.4 Wisdom and Compassion, Love and Justice

Buddhists as well as Christians say that much is wanting in the way in which people usually live in the world. For the most part, they agree on the reasons for this: egotism, attachment, and desire. I have already discussed the Buddhist view on the removal of the basic attachment to the self. This attachment inevitably brings with it not only suffering, but also ambiguity and a lack of discernment. Through one's attachment to oneself, one is no longer capable of discerning the true desires of oneself and others; one is no longer open to what people actually intend, and one certainly does not have a clear opinion as to what their true desires are. In society people often appeal to others and must determine whose wishes they will most often meet. People have their limits — they cannot do everything. In all these judgments someone else's ideals, desires, and self-image play a decisive role, adversely affecting the formation of such judgments. In principle everyone stands too much in their own way to see what is going on and to know really what is on someone else's mind. This is in addition to the fact that people do not know what they should talk about and what they should not talk about, what should be done or left undone, what is truly important to someone, or they are unable to come up with a proper compromise between different interests. In short, in order to see reality as it truly is, people must be detached in such a way that they are no longer attached to their (alleged) "self" and illusory images of reality. Most people achieve the related ideals of perception and detachment only through much practice and meditation. On this point Buddhists and Christians agree.

The truly emancipated existence is characterized by virtue. As we have seen, Buddhist ethics consists of the doctrine of virtues; it constantly involves a person's disposition.[55] The most important virtues in Buddhism are self-control, moderation, contentment, celibacy, patience, purity, humility, kindness, generosity, respect, thankfulness, tolerance, sincerity, and justice.[56] Love for one's neighbor is perfect

---

55. Bechert, "Historical Buddha," p. 299.

56. S. Tachibana, *The Ethics of Buddhism* (London: Curzon, 1926), p. 95. Cf. P. Gerlitz, "Die Ethik des Buddha: Philosophische Grundlagen und sittlichen Normen im Frühen Buddhismus," in *Ethik der Religionen: Ein Handbuch,* ed. C. H. Ratschow (Stuttgart: Kohlhammer, 1980), pp. 271-80.

only when one does not hate but loves both friend and foe equally. A ruler must be just; his or her rule must be characterized by impartiality, the giving of alms, honesty, integrity, and unpretentiousness.[57] Even ahimsa (nonviolence) is to be one of the ruler's characteristics.

The background for Buddhist ethics is the Buddhist view of reality, involving primarily two basic insights that mark Buddhist morality. The first is the doctrine of *anatman,* (no-self-hood). As we have seen, this doctrine differs from Christian belief, which in contrast confirms the human person: the new self emerges through emptying, although the old self still exists beside the new self. The second basic insight of Buddhism that defines morality is the "chain of causal relation." It begins with the idea that ignorance leads to the development of wrong dispositions, which in turn leads to experiencing things in the wrong way; the wrong experience of things ultimately leads to "thirst," either desire or attachment. Thus ignorance and attachment are directly linked with the wrong and so-called ordinary awareness of reality.[58] Reality is like a wheel that revolves, its movement causing the one to give rise to the other; all things cohere. Karma encompasses everything, nothing is left undetermined,[59] and for this reason one must learn to see oneself as a small part of the great whole. Everything that is, is part of this great field. One who lives in continuity with everything can regard the other as — in a sense — oneself. Nishitani tells the following story of two people who meet:

> Kyozan Ejaku asked Sansho Enen, "What is your name?"
> Sansho said, "Ejaku!"

---

57. Gerlitz, "Die Ethik des Buddha," pp. 322-23; cf. Tachibana, *Ethics of Buddhism,* p. 264.

58. See Gerlitz, "Die Ethik des Buddha," pp. 237-38, for more detail; cf. my *Religions and the Truth,* p. 154.

59. For a discussion of the question of (in)determinism, see D. J. Kalapuhana, *Buddhist Philosophy: A Historical Analysis* (Honolulu: University of Hawaii Press, 1976), pp. 50ff.; Kalapuhana posits that, according to Buddha, human actions are neither wholly determined nor wholly free (humans thus bear moral responsibility). Kalapuhana quotes the following on p. 51: "Action is the field, consciousness the seed, and craving the moisture which lead to the rebirth of a being" (*Anguttara-nikaya,* 5 vols., ed. R. Morris and E. Hardy [London: PTS, 1885-1900], 1:223-24). In my opinion, this gives rise to the problem that freedom, according to Mahayana Buddhism, is achieved by placing oneself in the position of *shunyata:* without the "great death" there is no freedom.

"Ejaku!" replied Kyozan, "that is *my* name."
"Well then," said Sansho, "my name is Enen."
Kyozan roared with laughter.[60]

If neither you nor I have an ego or even a name, then we have no lasting self that must be embraced and thus no identity to sustain. Because of this, the sharpness of the distinction between the one and the other fades. People are part of the same reality. On the one hand, this is the basis of equality between people; on the other hand, it is the basis of respect for the whole of nature: all of reality — everything that is — is part of the causal whole.[61]

To this experience of reality belong the virtues of wisdom and compassion *(karuna)*. Wisdom is discerning that which is really good for someone else and for "oneself" and which is also good within the total relation of things. Everything else is now seen "in truth" *(suchness):* equal in the great process of things; at the same time weaknesses and possibilities are clearly recognized. Compassion is correlated to the experience of emptiness: everything is part of the one great whole, the stream of events that has no fixed center (and in this sense is *emptiness*) and is both impressive and sufficient at the same time (and in this sense is *fullness*). Because the human "ego" lapses, all people, animals, and plants are experienced as elements of this relatedness, and one is filled with compassion equally for all. Most important are peace, wisdom, insight, appropriate actions, and compassion.

This view overlaps the Christian view on a number of points, particularly in the central position of the reorientation of the ego and in the critique of the so-called usual way of things in the world. Emphasis is laid on the equality of people. For Buddhists and Christians the so-called ordinary life is not at all ordinary; there is sufficient

60. K. Nishitani, "The I-Thou Relation in Zen Buddhism," in *Buddha Eye,* p. 48.

61. For emphasis on the importance of concern for nature, see the contributions of P. de Silva and Abe to the collection *Human Rights and Religious Values: An Uneasy Relationship,* ed. A. An-Na'im et al. (Grand Rapids: Eerdmans; Kampen: Kok Pharos, 1995). Buddhist thought is much less anthropocentric than Western and Western Christian thought. The practice of Buddhists' actions toward nature should not be viewed in a straightforward way; see L. Schmithausen, *Buddhism and Nature,* Studia Philologica Buddhica, Occasional Paper Series 7 (Tokyo: International Institute for Buddhist Studies, 1991).

evidence of many forms of evil. People have no self that they can burnish and use to justify themselves. Christianity has a strong relativization of personal merit. When someone does good, the Reformed tradition speaks of deeds of gratitude: they are not viewed as meritorious but as evidence of gratitude for the grace one has encountered. The greatest commandment is to love God; the second commandment, similar to the first, is to love one's neighbor as oneself. Thus Christianity also commends love of one's neighbor, justice, charity, and discernment.

The questions that a Christian must ask of the Buddhist view are closely related to the Christian confirmation of the value of people and the value of human relations. The reason that God created people has to do with his love. Because he wanted to express his love, he created people;[62] people are responsible creatures who can accept or reject God's love.[63] God's love reaches out to sinful people, and it is the confirmation of people through God's unconditional love that frees people to love their neighbor. As it is written in 1 John: "We love because he first loved us."[64]

From the Christian point of view love is always related to the confirmation of human identity: one can only love someone by acknowledging her or his otherness and integrity.[65] The relation to the other is at the same time constitutive for one's own identity. People find their identity among others, living in the world (as creation) before the

---

62. See Berkhof, *Christian Faith,* p. 152; K. Barth, "The Yes of God the Creator," in *Church Dogmatics,* III/1, ed. G. W. Bromiley and T. F. Torrance, tr. J. W. Edwards et al. (Edinburgh: T. & T. Clark, 1958), p. 382; H. Heppe and E. Bizer, *Die Dogmatik der evangelisch-reformierten Kirche: Dargestellt und aus den Quellen belegt* (Neukirchen: Neukirchener Verlag, 1958²), pp. 152, 156; according to the classical Reformed theologians, the ultimate purpose of creation is to honor God; goodness is the *cause* of creation.

63. And yet, viewed from another perspective, the believer confesses that God activates the will; cf. Phil. 2:13; on human freedom and mercy, cf. V. Brümmer, "Can We Resist the Grace of God?" in *Speaking of a Personal God: An Essay in Philosophical Theology* (Cambridge: Cambridge University Press, 1992), pp. 68-89.

64. 1 John 4:19.

65. Catherine Keller, "Scoop up the Water and the Moon Is in Your Hands: On Feminist Theology and Dynamic Self-Emptying," in *Emptying God,* p. 109, thus says correctly: "The self is not the self unless the other is the other . . . God is not God unless God is the other." For the theme of the other as fundamental to human existence, see Emmanuel Levinas.

face of God. Exchanging names, as the two Zen masters did, is inconceivable within the Christian tradition. Such an exchange does not correspond to the confirmation of human identity. A person's name is given at baptism; young parents often write on their birth announcements that the name of their child is written in the palm of God's hand. This is a fundamental difference between Buddhism and Christianity. It concerns another sort of relatedness, not of everything with everything, but the relation between people and the relation between people and nature, which leads to another issue. If the essence of Christian love lies in the fact that every person is known to God and that God first loved people, whereas Buddhist compassion *(karuna)* arises from and is paired with selflessness, then the question arises as to whether one may equate the *agape* (love) of the gospel with the Buddhist *karuna* (compassion). From a Buddhist viewpoint, I think that the Christian love of one's neighbor is evidence of attached living. Abe says explicitly: "Love is a positive attachment. Hate is a negative attachment"[66] — but all attachment, positive as well as negative, is problematic. Love entails pain — whereas we have seen how Abe believes that one can remain undisturbed by suffering from the perspective of *shunyata.* In Christianity one is permitted to be attached to whomever one loves. That is why death is, as Paul says, the last enemy, and there is nothing wrong with Jesus' grief at the death of Lazarus.[67]

The entire Bible is full of the ideal of the good life, and it is always a life conceived in terms of social relations. The prophets knew all about the perversion of love into a form of greed and the dangers of uncontrolled passion; but all the same, love is of paramount importance, including sexual relations between partners, in spite of the attachment and pain that relations inevitably cause. Parents are attached to their children and thereby are vulnerable. This corresponds to the Buddhist view: attachment entails vulnerability and leads to suffering. The Bible recognizes this, as can be seen in the story of David and Absalom. Yet the honest and just confirmation of each other's being a person precisely in being different is highly regarded in Christianity. This confirmation of the person does not involve self-exaltation and personal development, but service and the employment of gifts within the community.

66. Abe, "Emptiness Is Suchness," in *Buddha Eye,* p. 205.
67. John 11:35. Cf. Paul in 1 Cor. 15:26.

In this context I must return to the issue of the relativization of the distinction between good and evil. If all things are part of a causal whole, then are not the just and unjust people *equally* parts of the same whole? Ejaku and Sansho are — in a sense — interchangeable. If one of them was an obviously "bad" person and the other an obviously "good" person (more on that below), would they not then be just as interchangeable? Buddhist doctrine has an impressive morality, with a distinction made between right and wrong actions. But the problem remains as to how, within the whole of reality in which all things influence one another — and in which I, as it were, must and may (!) be submerged in a passing element (emptiness, the self as no-self), there can still be a fundamental difference between justice and injustice. As we have seen, Abe relativizes good and evil.[68] Much in the world is profane, unjust, and simply evil. How is it possible to take a clear position against injustice from within the chain of causality? Some Buddhist schools have a large political commitment, and this raises the question of how one relates the content of faith and the experience of salvation to morality (and not whether there are Buddhists with social commitment, for that is obvious).

In the meantime, one must realize that the emphasis which many Christian schools place on the distinction between justice and injustice is open to criticism from a Buddhist perspective. And because of this, Abe — with all respect for the Christian view — has indicated that the bid for a better world from the ideal of a good world inevitably leads to attachment and thus wrong behavior.[69] In this context, justice has two aspects: balancing between people and their desires on the one hand, and judgment and punishment on the other. Buddhism cannot admit justice in this last sense; it is a two-edged sword, Abe writes,

---

68. Cf. Abe, *Zen and Western Thought*, p. 191; cf. above; see also C. Anbeek, J. van Bragt, and E. Cornélis, *Voorbij goed en kwaad? Christendom en Boeddhisme* (Kampen: Kok, 1991); M. Van den Boom, "Boeddhisten en christenen in gesprek," in *Wereld godsdiensten in Nederland,* ed. J. Slomp (Amersfoort: De Horstink, 1991), p. 185: "The obsession with guilt, payment, sin, and morality is not known in Buddhism. The Abhidharma doctrine at least views these notions as characteristic of the state of mind of the unenlightened person in samsara. The belief in these notions ties the person to samsara. The person is 'depraved' in Buddhism — not in the sense that he or she is bad or disobedient, but in the sense that he or she is blind, shortsighted, and ignorant."

69. Abe, *Zen and Western Thought*, p. 183.

because such a reaction evokes a counterreaction that starts the cause-and-effect process.[70] Striving for justice apart from wisdom and the love of one's enemy often leads to harm and does in fact occur frequently. Thus, according to the Bible, one may not separate justice from compassion. Justice, judgment, punishment, and atonement are legitimate categories. From the Christian perspective one cannot endorse what Abe writes:

> In the final and deepest realization of the dilemma between good and evil, the structure of my ego collapses and I come to the realization that I am not simply good or simply bad. I am neither good nor bad. I am nothing whatsoever. However, this realization is not negative but positive, because in the full realization of Nothingness, we are liberated from the dichotomy of good and evil, life and death.[71]

Buddhism has no room for a God who desires justice, forgives sins and enters into a relation with people as a "partner" in history. Abe, who has a very good understanding of Christian belief, characterizes the difference itself as follows: for Buddhism what counts the most is the problem of death and life, whereas for Christianity the most important issue is what a person should do.[72] This characterization is too moralistic. Where the Spirit is, there is liberation; and the gospel concerns the liberation from the burden of existence, the forgiveness of all shortcomings, the victory over sin and death — in short, the good life.

2.5 The Truth of the Existence of Suffering

The differences mentioned between Buddhism and Christianity cohere with the different views of the cause of evil and ignorance. On the one hand, according to the Buddhist Noble Truth of the origin of suffering, suffering arises from greed, attachment, and ignorance;

70. Abe, "Rejoinder," p. 180.
71. Abe, *Zen and Western Thought,* p. 191.
72. Ibid., pp. 192, 272-73.

according to the Christian view, on the other hand, suffering comes from wanting to become a good person on one's own. In the biblical narrative of the Fall, the fundamental fault of Adam and Eve is their desire to be like God — "knowing good and evil."[73] It concerns the desire to be independent of God and to decide and to act for oneself: living not before the face of God *(coram Deo)* but out of oneself *(coram se ipso)*. This notion is central in Paul's writings:[74] the fundamental mistake that people make is wanting to make themselves good. In order to succeed in life they are willing to comply with ideals, habits, or laws. Some people try to "improve" themselves through fraud and crime. That is not good. Others are more clever: in order to "improve" themselves they comply with the rules, are generally respected, are sometimes promoted, and thus fulfill their desires. All people, both good and evil, are "under the law," as Paul writes. Paul believes that the most outstanding people are slaves of the law; he is thinking here of none other than the law-abiding Jewish people, like himself in his younger days. The root of all evil is that people think they can justify themselves or, in other words, that they can raise themselves to being good and successful people. They are unable to do this because the attempt entails an attachment to rules. In reality it is servitude, not freedom.

The law — no matter which one — is a yoke that leads to servitude. It does not matter which law or fine ideals one holds to, the law always becomes the master; it can never be fulfilled. I can never make myself into a completely good person. There are too many dangers, too many imperfections lurking; too much can interfere. I always fail somewhere. Moreover, the fine ideals and high norms have their own dynamic, which in the end turns against the person. The high ideals that must be achieved and rules that must be obeyed cause one to experience one's limits more strongly than without such high ideals and stringent norms. The law that is intended to make a good life possible has the opposite effect; as Paul writes: "when the commandment came, sin sprang to life and I died. I found that the very commandment that was intended to bring life actually brought death."[75] Laws, rules, and high

---

73. Gen. 3:5.

74. The classic expositions can be found in the letters to the Romans and Galatians. See Schmithals, *Die theologische Anthropologie des Paulus,* pp. 47-51.

75. Rom. 7:9-10.

ideals — although good in themselves — are not an antidote to sin. But what must people do then, if they do not want the world to end in chaos? What else is there but high ideals, intense efforts at what is good, and, where necessary, stringent laws?

I hope it is clear from the wording how close the Buddhist and Christian views are on this point. Suffering stems from the wrong orientation of the will and consciousness. But now the difference between the two becomes apparent. How can one refrain from wanting to succeed as a person? For Paul this involves a no-self, but he does not base this on a path that one must walk by oneself. With respect to the Buddhist way of removing suffering, the Eightfold Path, the Christian (and particularly Protestant) point of view raises the following question: Is the way of meditation, liberating insight, and detachment itself a means of escaping the cycle of life by letting go *of everything* and having compassion *for everything?* This would entail the consequence that in existence one is not dependent on relations with others, and the other is not actually valued as an other with an individual name, which would make us a neighbor and a responsible person. I mention here three points where the Buddhist removal of suffering differs from the Christian faith.

First, Christian faith is not concerned with removing suffering from the world in which we live or, as it is called, from this broken world. Following Christ entails suffering — even if only through insight into how things are: the brokenness of the world, the groaning of the creation, the yearning of all things for the children of God to be revealed, and the cry of the humiliated and wronged. Within the sphere of this world, Christian faith does not involve being unaffected by one's own suffering or that of others, but rather it involves conquering sin and its forms of expression. Abe writes that history teaches that the Buddhist doctrines of nirvana, *shunyata,* and the transcendence of all distinctions caused Buddhists to detach from concrete historical concern in the sense of involvement with social injustices and historical evils. He holds that Buddhism exhibits weaknesses here that must be amended.[76] For some individual Buddhists social justice has arisen as a by-product of the Buddhist doctrine of salvation,[77] but I think

---

76. Abe, "Rejoinder," p. 179.

77. This is how A. Pieris expresses it, referring to examples from *dalit*-literature in India (the *dalit* are the oppressed in India), in *Love Meets Wisdom: A Christian Experience of Buddhism* (Maryknoll, N.Y.: Orbis, 1988), p. 128.

that true social involvement is ultimately possible only if Buddhism also delays the removal of suffering to the eschaton, if it teaches people to become "attached" to that which is good and beautiful and to each other, and to worry about the oppressed and about those who suffer more than others. Perhaps the idea that liberation from samsara can be delayed by those who have achieved enlightenment in order to help others can be so interpreted that social justice more clearly becomes part of the Buddhist ethos.[78] But if we learn to view the world in this way, we do not avoid the question of whether people themselves can ever overcome suffering. We need help; and from who else but God?

A second difference is that, for Christian faith, the *suchness* of things (in their true nature) is not the relatedness of everything with everything but rather a varied and complex world of joy and sorrow, sacrifice and greed, support and abandonment, justice and injustice, love and selfishness. In this world things are related, but this is not the primary insight. Rather, the primary insight is how people enter into good or bad relations with their neighbors and with God and how they deal with nature; it concerns insight into life from the perspective of the kingdom of God.

The third difference relates closely to the above points. Christian faith holds that freedom lies at the beginning of the path.[79] It is a threefold path of faith, hope, and love. Love, justice, and mercy are not relative. The beginning of the Christian path is acceptance of the offer of grace in faith: God's unqualified, unconditional endorsement of our life. It is sinners, not good people, who are justified. Therefore sin and evil are not relative either. The only solution to the problem of self-justification, within which people irrevocably lock themselves, is that one need not make oneself good and acceptable. The gospel is the message that God loves sinners — failures, who therefore no longer need to make themselves "good" and can surrender themselves to God's love. This is what Christian freedom involves: one does not "have to" any longer. The law is no longer master. With God's acceptance one can live in freedom: one need no longer stand in one's own

78. This is the Bodhisattva ideal in Mahayana Buddhism; see E. Conze, *Buddhism: Its Essence and Development* (Oxford: Cassirer, 1951), pp. 127-30; cf. Pieris, "The Buddhist Political Vision," in *Love Meets Wisdom*, pp. 73-79.

79. See, among others, Rom. 3:9–8:39; Gal. 3:1–5:26; and 1 Corinthians 13.

way, and one is able to face all the facts (in their suchness) without any shrinking from them. Test everything, writes Paul, and hold on to the good.[80] Everything is permitted, but not everything is useful. This submission in faith is not an attitude that must be achieved or for which one must strive; it is simply humbly accepting that the individual, just as he or she is, finds grace in the eyes of God. It is not a requirement that one first free oneself from attachment and ignorance (by which one would still live for oneself), but one is allowed, within the great framework of God's kingdom, to be what one is. The essence of the gospel is that this simply happens to people: grace is freely given — one only has to experience it. For whoever actually does this, this faith bears its own fruit because such a person is free to see what can and should be done.[81] According to the Reformational understanding of faith, justification precedes sanctification.

There are still other questions to ask from a Christian perspective. A few well-known themes are related to what has been discussed, for example, the doctrine of reincarnation, which I discuss in chapter three.

The dialogue between Christians and Buddhists is exceptionally exciting; there is affinity on many points. Christians and Buddhists share many insights, although it is not easy to penetrate to the core of correspondence and difference of views. Time and again people can learn from each other. In the midst of secularization and the materialism of Western culture, the Christian churches can learn much from the Buddhist view with regard to personal spirituality. A true dialogue consists of critical questions as well as understanding and appreciation. I have mentioned a few of the most important points of difference, which, again, are starting points for further discussion.

80. 1 Thess. 5:21.
81. Cf. Heidelberg Catechism, a. 64: "It is impossible for those grafted into Christ by true faith not to produce fruits of gratitude." One might ask here how many "truly" believe, just as one might ask how many are truly "enlightened." For the relation between freedom and following norms, see Berkhof, *Christian Faith*, pp. 455-56.

3

God Has an Inexhaustible Number of Names

3.1 Introduction

In this chapter I discuss several ideas in Hindu traditions. As varied as these traditions are, the following ideas are fundamental: God has many names, and concealed behind all these names is that which is the highest, deepest, and most encompassing; human beings exist in connection with all things; each individual human life is part of a long series of lives. I examine primarily these fundamental ideas, which are widespread among diverse Hindu traditions. Also important is the unique nature of these — as they are called — "Eastern religions." Western religions are said to be more rigid in outlook and less contemplative and tolerant than Eastern religions. This is an important point, although such a distinction between "Western" and "Eastern" religions is far too general. There is much ritualism in some Eastern and Western traditions alike, with conventions and regulations sometimes playing a large role. Within the religions themselves there are significant differences, since each religion contains a number of groups with differing emphases. What does the cumbersome expression "the Eastern" or "the Western" religion(s) mean? All the world religions are of Asian origin. Both Hinduism and Buddhism originated in India, and Taoism and Confucianism emerged in China. The three monotheistic religions — Judaism, Christianity, and Islam — arose in Western Asia. One must not speak too quickly of Christianity as a Western religion. European — and subsequently North American — Christianity spread over the world, yet the majority of Christians live in parts of the world other than Europe or North America.

One cannot, therefore, begin with such a simple opposition between Eastern and Western religions. In *critical dialogue* particularly, one should shun such quick characterizations in order to avoid the danger of effectively removing any possibility of mutual criticism. It is, nevertheless, an important point. The history of Western culture has followed a particular direction that to a large degree determines what counts as happiness, true knowledge, and a high cultural level. This direction can be characterized by the terms "empiricism," "Enlightenment," and "technocracy/industry." The question is whether Western culture, as it has developed, is the best medium for a proper understanding of religion, including the gospel. Western individualism and the almost unbridled use of natural raw materials has been criticized by other cultures. In a truly critical dialogue Westerners must be attentive to what they can learn from the Eastern tradition.

The mode of thought in Middle and Eastern Asian religions, such as Hinduism, Buddhism, and Shinto, is often said to be less a matter of either/or and more one of both/and than the Semitic religions. The divine is described in inclusive language rather than in restrictive language. That which is most important cannot be unequivocally expressed; whatever is said requires that more be said: it is neither this nor that. The divine cannot be comprehended, let alone exhaustively described. More can and must be said about the divine, which accounts for the characteristic multiplicity of divine images and narratives. The number of gods and images of gods is impressive, even if one has only a limited knowledge of the Hindu myths and traditions or simply views the Hindu images in documentaries and travel guides. The piety of village rituals, the offerings in temples or on family altars, the abandonment and ecstasy in festivals — all these demonstrate how religion is interwoven with life as a whole. The many religious schools allow people to worship the divinity of their choice.[1] This is not to say that there are no limits as to what is permissible. Rites, such as those that must be observed with respect to marriage and burial, are described in detail.[2] The pandit is a person with knowledge of the rituals, and the

---

1. See, for example, A. van Dijk, "Hinduism," in *Religionen der Welt: Grundlagen, Entwicklung und Bedeutung in der Gegenwart,* ed. M. Tworuschka and U. Tworuschka (Gütersloh: Bertelsmann Lexikon Verlag, 1992), p. 270.

2. Cf. B. Faddegon, "Brahmanisme en Hindoeïsme," in *De godsdiensten der wereld,* ed. C. J. Bleeker (Amsterdam: Meulenhof, 1955³), pp. 224-38, on rituals. J. C.

order that he observes is directly related to the order (dharma) that is the foundation of the world itself. The rites are fixed and thus some things are excluded. Not everything is regarded equally and without further interpretation as true — tolerance also has its limits. The typical Hindu solution to the problem of someone who transgresses the rules is not ostracism from the culture but assignation to a lower status.[3] The establishment of limits entails a form of exclusivity, and we should therefore discuss that which is considered to be true and good.

In this chapter I examine two ideas of the Hindu tradition in particular. The greatest and most current challenge for modern Christianity lies in the Hindu idea that all things form one great encompassing whole. People do not stand over against nature but are included within it. All of reality contains a spark of the divine and is ultimately divine. If one can speak of "holism" anywhere, then it is here: reality ultimately forms a divine whole. This accounts for the abundant images of the divine: all aspects of existence must be depicted in connection with the Highest. The second Hindu idea I examine is the notion of reincarnation, along with the related notion of karma and its social-ethical implications.

3.2 The Many Images of the One Divinity

Divinity is inconceivable — it is too high and too large, too multifaceted and encompassing, and every conception of it is inadequate.

Heesterman emphasizes strongly that rituals, particularly some offerings, serve to preserve cosmic order. This is why the correct performance of rituals is so important. Cf. his "'I am who I am.' Truth and Identity in Vedic Ritual," in *Beiträge zur Hermeneutik indischer und abendländischer Religionstraditionen,* ed. G. Oberhammer (Vienna: Verlag der Oesterreichischen Akademie der Wissenschaften, 1991), p. 173; and his "Vedic Sacrifice and Transcendence" and "Ritual, Revelation, and the Axial Age," in *The Inner Conflict of Tradition: Essays in Indian Ritual, Kingship and Society,* ed. J. C. Heesterman (Chicago and London: University of Chicago Press, 1985), pp. 81-107.

3. J. F. Staal, "Über die Idee der Toleranz im Hinduismus," *Kairos* 1 (1959): 215-18; cf. also my *Religions and the Truth: Philosophical Reflections and Perspectives,* tr. J. W. Rebel (Grand Rapids: Eerdmans; Amsterdam: Rodopi, 1989), ch. 3, §4.

This notion allows two possibilities. First, one could either say that not too much should be said about the divine or, better yet, that *nothing* should be said about the divine since no one ever knows what the divine actually is. This is typical of Advaita mysticism: the divine is exalted above thought. It is only when one ceases to think and to speak that one approaches the truth. In principle, we cannot say the one (not-two: *advaita*), for we always speak with a multiplicity of words. The one truth is beyond words! For this reason all images and expressions must be transcended in a quiet union with the divine.

This type of mysticism is one way: orientation to the divine beyond all images and expressions. But one may also follow the path leading in the opposite direction: because the divine has an inexhaustible number of aspects, there is much that must be said and expressed, and the divine must be worshiped in many gods. This is typical of the countless religious traditions within the Hindu culture that have many temples and family altars. One should note that not only is the divine actually worshiped in many images, but it is *only* in these several ways that it can be worshiped, for it is itself multifaceted and inexhaustible and, at the same time, one.[4] The one that encompasses everything cannot be worshiped as a part and as "one"; as soon as it is conceived, there are "two" of it (something that one posits *before* oneself, thus over against oneself). That is why the one is represented in the many — in inexhaustible variety.

In order to receive a good impression of the varied world of the gods, one must sample that world. Images and pictures of gods can be viewed in museums,[5] and documentaries offer information on Hindu festivals. One can gain some idea of the multiplicity and complexity of Hindu myths by looking at one of the popular stories of a divinity. By way of example I will relate the story about the head of Ganesha, the god of wisdom and the helper in troubles, the lord of the armies of the great god Shiva. Ganesha is depicted as a relatively small, thickset divinity with four hands. His most remarkable feature is his head, which is that of an

4. See Diana L. Eck, *Darśan: Seeing the Divine Image in India* (Chambersburg, Penn.: Anima, 1981), pp. 17-22; cf. the eulogy of Devi on p. 21 of this work: "Nameless and Formless Thou art, O Thou Unknowable. All forms of the universe are Thine; thus Thou art known!"

5. In the Netherlands fine collections can be viewed at the Tropenmuseum and the Rijksmuseum in Amsterdam and the Volkenkundig Museum in Leiden. The Tropenmuseum also sells compact discs of the music of Eastern rituals.

elephant with one tusk. At his feet is his mount, a rat — an indication of the god's energy and character. He moves through obstacles like an elephant through the forest and like a rat biting its way into the granary. Thus Ganesha clears a way through the wilderness for all who worship him.[6] His four hands hold symbols that express his divine and individual characteristics. He is sometimes portrayed with a shell containing rice or pearls in one hand for the one to whom he is favorably disposed. Blessed is the one whom Ganesha favors; the Lord is near him or her, but the one from whom he turns away and shows his back should take heed. The front of the images show Ganesha as the well-disposed, helping god, but the back shows a fearful monster of another name — Kirttimukha, "the face of glory" — a protector for the faithful but filled with menace for the unfaithful.[7] Ganesha is the son of Shiva and Parvati. For his disciples Shiva is the lord of the universe, and he is often depicted as the dancing Shiva, the lord of the world who causes things to arise and to pass away. He is the god of *enlightenment (moksha)* and of destruction of ignorance. One of his consorts is the goddess Parvati, Ganesha's mother. There are various legendary accounts as to how the child lost his head and received an elephant's head. One of these accounts tells of how Parvati, proud of her son, asked Shani, the divinity of the planets, to look on her son, forgetting the consequences of the heavenly divinity's glance. He did what she asked, but burned off the child's head when he looked at him. The god Brahma advised Parvati to replace the head with the first head she could find. This was done and Ganesha's new head was that of an elephant.[8]

As one can expect in this genre, however, different versions of this story relate completely different accounts. In the version that I give here one can see the transitions made between the divinities and the divine powers, through which it becomes clear how the multifaceted divine reality appears in alternating aspects. Both Shiva and Parvati are referred to by more than one name. The mysterious, mighty reality that, replete with antagonistic powers, forms the whole

---

6. H. Zimmer, *Myths and Symbols in Indian Art and Civilization,* ed. J. Campbell, Bollingen Series 6 (Princeton: Princeton University Press, 1946, reprint 1974), pp. 70, 183.

7. Ibid., p. 184.

8. *Lexikon der östlichen Weisheitslehren,* ed. S. Schuhmacher and G. Woerner (Bonn: Scherz, 1986), p. 119.

of existence is presented in a narrative way. In these stories the all-too-human is combined with the mysterious, the "this-worldly" with the "otherworldly." The fundamental connections that exist among things are thus shown to be many sided, complex, and surprising. The story has a unique power that transcends argument: it evokes the complex reality without being able to understand it completely. Everything that is said requires supplementation, for reality is multifaceted and beyond human comprehension. In order to clarify this, I provide a shortened version of Ganesha's story as it is included in a selection of Hindu myths by Cornelia Dimmitt and Jan van Buitenen. One should note that the gods are sometimes referred to by more than one name.

Once upon a time while Pārvatī was taking a bath, the always auspicious Śiva threatened Nandin, who was guarding her door, and went into the house. When that lovely woman, the mother of the world, saw Śankara arrive so unexpectedly, she stood up, embarrassed. After this happened, the auspicious Pārvatī, supreme Māyā, the supernal goddess, became eager to follow the good advice given earlier by a friend, thinking to herself, "I should have a servant of my very own! He should be favorable to me, a man of accomplishment who will obey my command and no other, one who will not stray even a hair's breadth from my side!"

Thinking these thoughts, the goddess fashioned from the dirt of her body a young man who possessed all these good characteristics. He was handsome, flawless of limb, sturdy, well-adorned, and most valorous and strong. She gave to him various garments, abundant ornaments, and an incomparable blessing. "You are my very own son!" she said, "I have no one else here who is mine alone."

At her words, the youth bowed and said to Śivā [= Pārvatī, Śiva's consort], "What task have you found for me? I shall do as you tell me." Thus addressed, Śivā answered her son, "Dearest son, hear my words. From now on you shall be my doorkeeper. You are my very own child; I have no one whatsoever but you who belongs to me. Let no one enter my house without my permission, my son, no matter who, no matter where. Use force if necessary, dear son. I mean this truly!" And so speaking, she gave him a hard stick, O seer. Gazing at his handsome body, she was thrilled with delight.

Then she kissed his face lovingly, embraced him with affection, and stationed him, staff in hand, at her door as chief of her *gaṇas* [guards]. And the great heroic *gaṇa,* stood at the door of her house, holding the staff in his hand, out of desire to please Pārvatī. After she had put her son Gaṇeśa, lord of the *gaṇas,* in front of her door, Śivā herself stayed inside to bathe with her companions.

At that moment Śiva, skilled in various sports, arrived eagerly at the door, O lion among seers. Not knowing he was lord Śiva, Gaṇeśa said, "You may not enter here, O god, without permission of my mother who is inside bathing. Where do you think you're going? Get out at once!" Saying this, Gaṇeśa brandished his staff to stop Śiva.

Looking at him, Śiva said, "You silly fool, who are you to keep me out? Don't you recognize me, stupid? I am none other than Śiva himself!" But Gaṇeśa struck the great lord of many sports with his stick. This infuriated Śiva who said once again to his son: "You are an imbecile not to know me! I am Śiva, the husband of Pārvatī, daughter of the mountain! I shall go into my own house, idiot. Why are you standing in my way?"

After the god had spoken, Gaṇeśa grew angry with Maheśa, who was going into the house, O brahmin, so he hit him again with his staff. At this Śiva became enraged. Mustering his own *gaṇas,* he asked them, "Who is this person? What is he up to? What is going on here, *gaṇas,* while you just stand there and watch?" . . .

[The *gaṇas* tried to persuade Gaṇeśa to let Śiva through. Śiva could not turn back now without losing face: his wife could interfere with his actions! Thus Śiva said:]

"Now the mountain daughter will reap the fruit of her act! . . . Wage all-out war. Let it come out as it will!" . . .

When Gaṇeśa saw the eminent *gaṇas* approaching, armed for battle, he said to them, "Come if you will, all you lords of the *gaṇas* following Śiva's command! I am only one boy who obeys the order of Śiva. Nevertheless, the goddess Pārvatī shall witness the strength of her son, while Śiva shall see the power of his own *gaṇas*! The fight that is about to take place between a child and mighty men is a contest between Bhavānī [Śivā] and Śiva. You are skilled in warfare, since you have fought before; I am a boy who has never been to battle. Nevertheless, I shall put you to shame in this conflict between the mountain-born woman and Śiva!" . . .

[And so the fighting began. Nandin and the others had no chance against the son of the goddess, who hit them away from the door with his iron-stubbed club. They were wounded and fled like deer who see a lion. Even Śiva, who stood in the middle of his troops, realized that this boy could only be overcome by means of a trick.]

Then all the gods and Maheśa's *gaṇas* were delighted to see both Śiva, embodied with qualities, and Viṣṇu come to the battle. Greeting each other with affection, they all celebrated. And Gaṇeśa, the heroic son of *śakti,* with his staff, following the way of heroes, was the first to worship Viṣṇu who brings happiness to all.

[Viṣṇu and Śiva prepared a trick to kill Gaṇeśa. Śiva attacked him with a trident, but Gaṇeśa struck him in the hand with his spear. Again he dispersed the *gaṇas,* so that Viṣṇu acknowledged that he was a great warrior, a great hero in the fight. Viṣṇu also joined in the fight. With the help of higher powers, Viṣṇu was not wounded by Gaṇeśa's club.]

Once again, . . . [Gaṇeśa] took up his matchless staff and struck Viṣṇu with it. Unable to withstand the blow, Viṣṇu fell to the ground. But he sprang up at once and battled again. . . . Seizing his opportunity at last, the trident-wielding Śiva . . . cut off the head of Gaṇeśa with his trident. When Gaṇeśa lost his head, both the army of the *gaṇas* and the army of the gods stood stock still, rooted to the earth.

After Gaṇeśa was killed, the *gaṇas* held a great festival to the sound of hand drums and kettle drums. Śiva was sorry that he had cut off Gaṇeśa's head, but the mountain-born goddess Pārvatī was furious: "What will I do? Where will I go? Alas, alas, misery engulfs me. . . . All the gods and *gaṇas* have killed my son. I shall wreak utter havoc! I shall bring about the dissolution of the world!"

Grieving in this manner, the great goddess of the universe, enraged, fashioned in an instant hundreds of thousands of *śaktis,* or powers. Once created, they bowed to the mother of the world, blazed forth and said, "O Mother, tell us what to do!" . . . She who is Prakṛti, full of fury, answered them all. "O *śaktis,* O goddesses, you are to annihilate the world without a moment's pause. O my companions, devour with a vengeance the gods, sages, . . . my very own followers and all the rest as well!"

At her command, all the *śaktis,* consumed with rage, prepared to destroy all the gods and other creatures. . . . No matter where one looked, there were the *śaktis!* . . . and they all snatched up the gods in their hands and hurled them into their open mouths.

50

Witnessing this devastation, Hara, Brahmā, Hari, Indra and all
the rest of the gods, *gaṇas* and seers said to themselves, "What is
this goddess doing, this untimely annihilation of the world?" Thus
they were uncertain and lost hope for their own lives. Gathering
together, they conferred with each other, saying, "We must consider
what to do. . . . Only when the mountain goddess is satisfied will
peace return to the world, and not otherwise, not even with a myriad
efforts! Even Śiva, skilled in all sports, the deluder of the world, is
filled with sorrow like the rest of us!"

A million gods were annihilated while Śiva was enraged; none
could prevail. There was no one whatsoever to withstand the mountain-born goddess, O seer, whether her own devotee or that of
another, whether god or Dānava, *gaṇa* or guardian of the quarters,
whether Yakṣa, Kinnara or seer, not even Viṣṇu, Brahmā or lord
Śankara himself! . . . All the gods were terrified and retreated to
some distance away.

Meanwhile Nārada of divine sight arrived — you, O seer — to
benefit the gods and *gaṇas*. After bowing to Brahmā, Viṣṇa, Śankara
and myself, he met with them and spoke, reflecting on what was
to be done. All the gods conferred with the great souled Nārada,
saying in unison, "How can our suffering be ended?" To this he
replied, "As long as the mountain-born goddess is without compassion, you will be miserable. Make no mistake about this!"

And then the seers headed by Nārada went to Śiva and all pro-
pitiated her in order to appease her fury. . . . Placating her with
devotion, they said to her, at the command of the gods and *gaṇas:*

"O Mother of the world, praise be to you! To you, Śivā! Glory
be to you, Candikā, to Kalyāṇī, praise! O Mother, you are the
primordial *śakti,* creatress of everything. You are the power that
protects, the power that destroys! O goddess, be content! Be serene!
Glory be to you, O goddess! The triple world is destitute because
of your rage!"

Thus hymned by the seers led by Nārada, the supreme goddess
continued to look furious and spoke not a word to them. So all the
seers bowed again to her lotus feet and spoke diplomatically once
more to Śiva with devotion, their hands folded in reverence:

"Forgive us, O goddess! Devastation is upon us! Your master
stands before you, Ambikā, look at him! We are the gods Viṣṇu,
Brahmā and the others, O goddess. We are your very own creatures

who stand before you with our hands folded in worship. Forgive us our fault, supreme goddess! All of us are utterly miserable. O Śivā, grant us peace!"

So speaking, all the seers, wretched and confused, stood together in front of Candikā with their hands folded in obeisance. When she heard what they said, Candikā grew pleased. And she answered those seers with a mind filled with compassion: "If you can revive my son, I shall stop my devastation. If you honor him and make him overseer of everything, then there will be peace in the world. In no other way will you be happy again."

Thus addressed, all the seers led by Nārada went to tell the gods what had happened. . . . All the miserable gods . . . folded their hands, and related it all to Śankara. At their words, Śiva said, "Do whatever is necessary to benefit the worlds. Go to the north and cut off the head of whomever you first encounter. After doing this, join that head to Gaṇeśa's body."

All this was done. . . . They brought the body, washed it by the rules and worshiped it. Then turning their faces to the north, they went out. The first thing they met was an elephant with a single tusk. Taking its head, all the deities fastened it firmly to the body of Gaṇeśa. Worshiping Śiva, Viṣṇu and Brahmā, they bowed and said, "We have done as you told us. Now you must finish the task." . . .

Again Brahmā, Viṣṇu and the gods bowed to their master, the lord who is without characteristics, god Śiva himself, and said, "Since all of us were born from your *tejas,* or energy, now let your *tejas* enter this body by means of the recitation of Vedic *mantras!*" And calling Śiva to mind, they all sprinkled blessed holy water on the corpse while reciting *mantras.* At the mere touch of the drops of water, Gaṇeśa regained both consciousness and life. . . . He was handsome, noble and resplendent, with a pleasing shape, a jolly manner and a ruddy elephant head.

Everyone rejoiced, their sorrows banished, O lord of seers, at the sight of Śivā's son restored to life. Filled with happiness, they showed him to the goddess. When she saw her son alive, she too was overcome with joy.[9]

9. *Classical Hindu Mythology: A Reader in the Sanskrit Purāṇas,* ed. and tr. Cornelia Dimmitt and J. A. B. van Buitenen (Philadelphia: Temple University Press, 1978), pp. 179-85.

This colorful story gives some insight into the discussion on God in the Hindu tradition. It is multifaceted: the gods know desires, love, and anger, and the one divine essence cannot be realized in one concept! The divine is represented in the divinities, whose mutual relationships change. Who is supreme? Is it Shiva? At the end he is called supreme, higher even than Brahma and Vishnu, but then he is at the same time "the lord without characteristics." But at the beginning of the story he is the quick-tempered lover who intends to have his way with his consort, who wishes to be able to bathe undisturbed. Who has the final say? Is it the primal source from whose energy all things are made, or the goddess of the mountains whose powers sustains all things and is able to destroy them? Who is the source of all things: Shiva the master without characteristics, or Parvati, the Mother, the goddess who has created all things and in her fury and grief becomes destructive? The order among the gods of the Hindu heaven is not clear. Sometimes they are depicted as one divinity with two heads or as an image with the faces of Brahma, Shiva, and Vishnu.[10] Still other images depict Shiva and his consort together, beside each other, or as an image with two sides — one female and the other male. Ultimately, all things are one.

In the Hindu traditions that worship Shiva or Shakti, the oneness of all things is symbolized in the more profound unity behind and in the polarity of male and female.[11] A widespread use of imagery of Shiva and Parvati is the stylized imagery of the male and female symbols: a flat female symbol *(yoni)* with the phallic symbol (the *linga*) rising from it. It is sprinkled with water or adorned with garlands of flowers. In the background is the idea that all things arise from the one that is without form and at bottom continue to participate in it. This unity of everything that exists is represented in images and myths by phallic symbols and sexual intercourse. The creator-god is depicted as rising from the upper part of an opened *linga*.

This image — the godhead having almost freed himself from a rock

---

10. A portrayal of Harihara (Vishnu on the left, Shiva on the right) from the Guimet Museum (Paris; Phnom Da style, Khmer area) in *Asian Art,* ed. B. S. Myers and T. Copplestone, rev. ed. (London: Hamlyn, 1987), p. 140, no. 54.

11. H. von Stietencron, "World and Deity: Conceptions of the Hindus: Hindu Perspectives," in H. Küng et al., *Christianity and the World Religions,* tr. P. Heinegg (Garden City, N.Y.: Doubleday, 1986), pp. 191-92; J. Gonda, *Die Religionen Indiens,* vol. 1: *Veda und älterer Hinduismus* (Stuttgart: Kohlhammer, 1960), pp. 257, 259.

— refers to another myth. While both Vishnu and Brahma in the beginning claimed to have created the world, Shiva appeared to them in the form of an enormous rock, to which no end could be discovered after a hundred years. Only after they had acknowledged Shiva's supremacy did the rock open and Shiva reveal himself as the "lord of the *linga*."[12] The rock is the symbol of the origin of everything; the cosmic *linga* encompasses all things. The powers and energies of sexuality and fruitfulness symbolize the energy that the whole of the universe possesses. The union of the male and female is one symbol of the encompassing unity of all things. The divine rises above worldly phenomena and oppositions, of which it is, at the same time, the ultimate ground. After all, the divine sustains the whole of reality, not only good but also evil, as is visible in Parvati's fury. The water drops that bring Ganesha to life symbolize holy water. The water of the great rivers in India is holy, and this holiness is concentrated in the holy river, the Ganges.[13]

Reality is ultimately one: divine energy that manifests itself in the multiplicity of that which exists. This oneness is depicted as multiplicity: the many gods and divinities are aspects of the supreme, the mysterious reality that escapes all human comprehension. Because the supreme is encompassing and inconceivable and because the divine is the ultimate ground of all reality and therefore all things are to some degree divine, the divine is acknowledged and worshiped in many forms.[14] Thus more than one path leads to the divine, and one is able to choose the family to which one wishes to belong: the family of Vishnu, of Shiva, of Parvati/Durga, or any of the many others. The God that one honors is worshiped as the supreme God. Each of the great gods represent the one divine. The images of gods are worshiped in the hope that the divinity will see the worshiper, will look on him or her in mercy. They are ultimately one. At the basis of all things is the *brahman,* the primal ground, the origin and goal of all creatures, omnipresent, infinite, the

12. Cf. Zimmer, *Myths and Symbols,* pp. 128-30, with ill. 30; *Classical Hindu Mythology,* pp. 205-6; L. P. van den Bosch, *Levende godsdiensten,* vol. 1: *Inleiding in het hindoeïsme* (Heerlen: Open Theologisch Onderwijs, 1990), p. 78. Zimmer also supplies a Cambodian illustration in which the goddess rises from an opened *linga,* p. 199, no. 64.

13. See D. L. Eck, *Banaras: City of Light* (New York: Knopf, 1982), pp. 211-15.

14. On multiplicity and unity of images of gods, see Eck, *Darśan,* pp. 17-22. This is also called kathenotheism: even though more than one god is worshiped, the divinity that is worshiped at a specific moment is worshiped as one god (pp. 19ff.).

only power in the universe, transcending all distinctions — even that of good and evil.[15] That which is one without characteristics or attributes is known in many ways, and therefore the divine is worshiped in many ways and the one is worshiped in the many.

It is therefore understandable that some Hindu schools like the Advaita Vedanta have abandoned the worship of the divinities. It is possible to be Hindu without believing in (a) God. A person then orients her- or himself completely toward the whole of reality, this world as viewed from the perspective of its ultimate ground. The one and the many go hand in hand; the divine can be worshiped in more than one way, even without images of gods and myths. Because the divine is inexhaustible as well as without characteristics, a person may worship one of the many divinities, but one is also free to abandon such worship. With this introduction to the idea on the divine in Hindu traditions by way of Ganesha's story, I shift to the discussion of some fundamental aspects of belief.

3.3 World Order, Duty, and Sanctity

Reality is ultimately seen as a whole. In their ignorance people do not see that they are essentially one with the primordial ground from which everything originates. By means of a magical power *(maya),* as it were, people perceive the world differently than what it actually is — an independent existence with a multiplicity of beings. In fact, reality is permeated with divine powers. Just as water makes life possible, so divinity flows through all things with the power of life. That which is unique about human beings, what they essentially are, is part of the divine, just as drops are part of the sea. "These rivers flow, the eastern toward the east, the western toward the west. They go just from the ocean to the ocean. They become the ocean itself. . . . there they know not 'I am this one,' 'I am that one.'"[16] This obtains for all that exists:

15. Gonda, *Religionen Indiens,* 1:265; Gonda continues: "its effect, however, is autonomous and automatic. It has no ethical character and is beyond good and evil."
16. Chandogya Upanishad, 6.11, in *A Source Book in Indian Philosophy,* ed. S. Radharkrishan and C. A. Moore (Princeton: Princeton University Press, 1973[5]), p. 69.

All creatures here, though they have come forth from Being, know not "We have come forth from Being." Whatever they are in this world, whether tiger, or lion, or wolf, or boar, or worm, or fly, or gnat, or mosquito, that they become.

    That which is the finest essence — this whole world has that as its self. That is Reality. That is *Atman*.

This awareness of being part of the great whole implies that reality has two aspects: life in this world and life beyond this world, the temporary and the eternal, the changing and the permanent. Those who are wise have found a solid foundation.

The wise one [that is, the Atman, the Self] is not born, nor dies.
This one has not come from anywhere, has not become anyone.
Unborn, constant, eternal, primeval, this one
Is not slain when the body is slain.[17]

The body is the chariot of the soul.[18] This view allows various possibilities for connecting religion and everyday life, which can be divided into three levels of religiosity.[19] Popular religion is primarily concerned with survival and improving one's existence. The gods are worshiped, called on for aid, and thanked; rites and festivals play a large role. At issue here is earthly welfare. A second level of experiencing religion is concern for a good reincarnation. Third, one can conceive of ultimate unity and the eternal together in such a way that this unity can be achieved only by detaching oneself from this world; religion is then directed toward overcoming attachment and the pure fulfillment of one's duties, unless one retires from the community at a more mature age and leads a solitary existence with the purpose of realizing the divine.

    The notion of the unity of all things as an expression of the one divine admits the distinction between good and evil. After all, the world is *not absolutely* identical with the brahman, the divine, but rather *fundamentally* or *at bottom*. The words "fundamentally" and "at bottom" entail an important restriction. We have already seen that

17. Katha Upanishad 2.18, in *Source Book,* p. 45.
18. Katha Upanishad 3.3, in *Source Book,* p. 46.
19. Van den Bosch, *Levende godsdiensten,* pp. 71-72.

the world is a manifestation of the one divine, and is created. This creation, however, is a "game" *(lila)* of the gods. The world does not seem to be what it is. Although it is ultimately one with brahman, it seems to be separate from it. If the divine is pure bliss, the world is that least of all. The world originated from a magical act, as it were; it is maya. The term *maya* has been translated as "illusion," but then it does not concern normal illusion. Here "illusion" does not mean that the world is not real and simply a figment of the human imagination. "Maya" means that the world is not as it seems; the world that one experiences is misleading as far as its true nature is concerned. At bottom, everything is one; but it appears in an actual multiplicity that is all too real.[20] By distinguishing between real and apparent reality, one is able to distinguish between good and evil. A powerful example of this is to be found in the way of life of the *samnyasin* — those who give up everything in this world and retreat to the woods.[21]

One can behave better or worse in everyday life as well. Whoever does not achieve enlightenment *(jivanmukti)*[22] in this life — something reserved only for a very few — is born again as a living creature: "He, however, who has not understanding, /Who is unmindful and ever impure, /Reaches not the goal, /But goes on to transmigration."[23] Thus reincarnation refers to an almost endless series of lives, in which the quality of former lives determines the next life. One reaps what one sows. "According as one acts, according as one conducts himself, so does he become. The doer of good becomes good. The doer of evil becomes evil."[24] I discuss belief in reincarnation in the following section (§3.4). The balance of good and evil deeds is called *karma*, "the supra-ethical impersonal system within which one's current situation

20. Cf. J. F. Staal, *Advaita Vedanta and Neoplatonism* (Madras: University of Madras, 1961), p. 122, who describes maya as "magically creative activity."

21. This is also the way of the Hindu mystic; for examples see A. Bancroft, *Weavers of Wisdom: Women Mystics of the Twentieth Century,* tr. W. M. J. Meissner-Stibbe (Arkana: Mirananda, 1989), pp. 73-83, 135-46.

22. Cf. G. Oberhammer, "Shankara's Teaching on Emancipation during One's Life," *SID* 2 (1992): 67-81.

23. Katha Upanishad, ch. 3, in *Source Book,* p. 33.

24. Brihadaranyaka Upanishad 4.4, in *Source Book,* p. 87; and in G. Dietz-Sontheimer, "Die Ethik des Hinduismus," in *Ethik der Religionen: Ein Handbuch,* ed. C. H. Ratschow (Stuttgart: Kohlhammer, 1980), p. 357.

in the world is regarded as fruit of the seeds sown by someone's behavior and attitude in the past, and the vision that similar seeds lie in all of the current activities which will continue to determine someone's life if he bears their fruits in the future."[25] It is clear that everything depends on which good and bad deeds are done. How does one acquire merit? How does evil accumulate?

To answer these questions one must distinguish two lines: first, that of duties, dharma, and the caste system; and second, that of the orientation to the brahman. The caste system is a religious order of the community. This societal order consists of four levels and those who fall outside them (referred to as "untouchables" or "outcasts"), as well as the Adivasi, members of ancient tribal cultures. Within the four levels are innumerable castes, distinguished by the duties they perform within their local culture. The word for "caste" is *jati*, which J. Gonda defines as "birth and form of being, rank and the belonging to a class or sort as determined by birth."[26] The duties and rights of every caste are arranged within the religious social system. Everything is part of a necessary order, which is religious in nature — the dharma, the cosmic order that permeates and orders all things.[27] The rituals performed by the brahmin as well as the deeds of other people are expected to fall within this order.

By birth people belong to a particular group or caste that performs

---

25. W. K. Mahony, "Karman: Hindu and Jain Concepts," in *The Encyclopedia of Religion,* ed. M. Eliade et al. (London: Macmillan, 1987), 8:262.

26. Gonda, *Religionen Indiens,* 1:297.

27. M. Biardeau, *Hinduism: The Anthropology of a Civilization,* tr. R. Nice (Delhi: Oxford University Press, 1981), p. 41: "it [dharma] is neither morality, nor good, nor law, nor justice. It is the socio-cosmic order, which . . . is necessary to the maintenance of the happy existence of the whole." Cf. also M. von Brück, "Sharing Religious Experience in Hindu-Christian Encounter," in *On Sharing Religious Experience,* ed. J. D. Gort et al. (Amsterdam: Rodopi; Grand Rapids: Eerdmans, 1992), p. 141: "The caste order, which is the very representation of the creational order"; Dietz-Sontheimer, "Die Ethik des Hinduismus," p. 404, gives the derivation of dharma: the root *dhr* means "maintain, support." See Rig Veda 10.90, as quoted by Wesley Ariarajah, "The Rise of the Dalit-Consciousness and Hindu-Christian Dialogue," *SID* 2 (1992): 102: "When they divided the *Purusa,* into how many parts did they arrange them? What was his mouth? What were his two arms? What are his thighs and feet called? The *brahmin* was his mouth, his two arms were made the *rajanya* (warrior), his two thighs the *vaisya* (trader and the agriculturist), from his feet the *sudra* (the servant) was born." See *Source Book,* p. 19.

specific duties and tasks in the whole community. One's caste determines whom one may marry or to whom one may be given in marriage, and the contacts that one may have within society in general. The caste system is hierarchical,[28] and this hierarchy is based primarily on the distinction between pure and impure and only secondarily on power and wealth. The "highest" *class* (consisting of many *castes*), although in economic terms it may be quite poor, is that of the brahmins, who are responsible for performing the rituals. The class of "warriors" *(Kshatriya varna)* has political and economic power, yet is less "high" than the brahmin. The castes have duties, with each caste performing tasks for society as a whole.[29] Duties are primarily the obligations of groups toward other groups, not rights of individuals. (The concept of individuality that is more or less basic to Western culture does not appear in India.) The individual is merely a unit within one's group, caste, or circle of relatives, which determines one's place in the hierarchy. Society is part of the cosmos. The person is special within this cosmos when the person has tasks that uphold the cosmic order. According to M. Biardeau, the meaning of human existence does not lie in being human as such, but rather is borrowed from the cosmic order and the place that the person has in it.[30] An individual's merit lies primarily in whether one carries out one's duties well. One compensates for breaches of the dharma through offering and purification. The purity of the class responsible for the rituals, the brahmins, is shown particularly by the distance that the outcastes must maintain from them and the high place in the hierarchy of those who are allowed to prepare their food.[31] The religious nature of the system is strongly apparent from the fact that, as stated above, the highest class is certainly not the richest. Princes and merchants can accumulate riches; brahmins can be very rich, but also very poor.

28. L. Dumont, *Homo Hierarchicus: The Caste System and Its Implications,* tr. M. Sainsbury (London: Weidenfeld and Nicholson, 1970), p. 107, passim. See also J. Massey, *Roots: A Concise History of the Dalits* (New Delhi: Indian SPCK, 1991).

29. Dumont, *Homo Hierarchicus,* on the "jajmani-system," pp. 97ff.

30. Biardeau, *Hinduism,* pp. 120, 160-61. Cf. Dietz-Sontheimer, "Die Ethik des Hinduismus," p. 392: fulfillment of reciprocal obligations does not fit into the Western idea of equality and striving for an equally high standard of living for all.

31. Dumont, *Homo Hierarchicus,* pp. 130-51. The ideal way of life for the brahmin is similar to that of those who retreat from society in order to attain emancipation; see J. C. Heesterman, "Brahmin, Ritual, and Renouncer," in *Inner Conflict of Tradition,* p. 43.

Thus the social hierarchy is not primarily determined by possessions or social success but by the socioreligious order of society. Here is an interesting example of the way the caste system works. In a particular area a number of people of a low caste became Christians. According to the dharma of their caste, they had to carry an image of the godhead worshiped through the village for an annual festival. They refused because of their Christian belief, yet the brahmins did not agree that they — regardless of their beliefs — should not fulfill their duties.[32] Thus the categories of good and evil are primarily related to the duties people have within the whole of reality.

This order of society also includes prescribed conduct that would be called morality. On the basis of the Bhagavad Gita, the fulfillment of duties with only the completion of the individual task in mind is seen as the highest virtue: "Therefore, without attachment, perform always the work that has to be done, for man attains to the highest by doing work without attachment."[33] From the entire conversation between Sri Krishna and Arjuna, in which Krishna speaks these words, it is clear just how much the fulfillment of the duties can conflict with prima facie obligations. Initially Arjuna refuses to begin the fight with his relatives and teachers: "It is better to live in this world by begging than to slay these honoured teachers. Though they are mindful of their gains, they are my teachers, and by slaying them, I would enjoy in this world delights which are smeared with blood."[34]

This basis for the resistance to fulfilling the *dharma* on the basis of prima facie obligations is negated by Sri Krishna by referring to the deeper being of people and the world:

11b. Wise men do not grieve for the dead or for the living.

12. Never was there a time when I was not, nor thou, nor these lords of men, nor will there ever be a time hereafter when we shall cease to be.

16. Of the non-existent there is no coming to be; of the existent

---

32. J. Carman, "Duties and Rights in Hindu Society," in *Human Rights and the World's Religions,* ed. L. S. Rouner (Notre Dame: University of Notre Dame Press, 1988), pp. 114ff.

33. Bhagavad Gita 3.19, in *Source Book,* p. 114. Other references to authoritative writings can be found in Dietz-Sontheimer, "Die Ethik des Hinduismus," pp. 401-2.

34. Bhagavad Gita 2.5, in *Source Book,* p. 106.

there is no ceasing to be. The conclusion about these two has been perceived by the seers of truth.

19. He who thinks that this slays and he who thinks that this is slain; both of them fail to perceive the truth; this one neither slays nor is slain.
20. He is never born, nor does he die at any time, nor having once come to be does he again cease to be. He is unborn, eternal, permanent, and primeval. He is not slain when the body is slain.
22. Just as a person casts off worn-out garments and puts on others that are new, even so does the embodied soul cast off worn-out bodies and take on others that are new.[35]

One's duties must be performed placidly and regardless of the consequences. Where the caste system is observed, these duties are the duties of the caste to which one belongs:

35. Better is one's own law though imperfectly carried out than the law of another carried out perfectly. Better is death in the fulfilment of one's own law, for to follow another's law is perilous.[36]

One can see here how metaphysics and the concept of humanity are interwoven with ethics. The notions of the dharma, which sustains everything, the duties it determines, and the idea of the continuing Self in the person (who is related to the divine) throughout the cycles of reincarnation, are completely determinative for the Hindu view of human existence, the relationships between people and their mutual contacts. The notions of karma and reincarnation (more on this in §3.4) are connected to the individual.[37] The "person" goes her or his own way through subsequent lives, but is at the same time part of the great whole. Because of this, the notion of individuality differs here from that of Western individualism.

Modern developments have caused changes in the caste system.

---

35. Bhagavad Gita from ch. 2, in *Source Book,* pp. 107-8.
36. Bhagavad Gita 3.35, in *Source Book,* p. 115; R. Fernhout, "Combatting the Enemy: The Use of Scripture in Gandhi and Godse," in *Human Rights and Religious Values: An Uneasy Relationship?* ed. A. An-Na'im et al. (Amsterdam: Rodopi; Grand Rapids: Eerdmans, 1995), pp. 120-32, describes how Godse, although a brahmin, was able to defy this rule in Gandhi's murder.
37. Heesterman, "Brahmin, Ritual, and Renouncer," p. 35.

Urbanization and "westernization" have decreased the importance of the ritual element in the caste system, and legislation is oriented toward lessening discrimination against the untouchables.[38] There are also indications that although the idea of (im)purity has lost its meaning for the caste system in some areas, the contrast pure/impure as an ethical direction still remains normative for the individual.[39] Where the caste system has slightly decreased in importance, the basic insights of the eternal Self, reincarnation, and the unity of all things in the one remain fundamentally determinative for the experience of reality. As far as the disappearance of castes is concerned, one must also take into consideration the difference in situation from region to region. The old structures and ideas continue to be strong in rural areas particularly.[40] Radical social changes need time. The continued opposition among social groups evokes sharp protest from the so-called *dalit* theology — the (Christian) theology of the untouchables. These protests serve as reminders that the caste system is still very much in effect. Duties and opportunities are still decisively determined by birth within a particular caste. It is said that a religious ideology lies at the root of the caste system,[41] and this includes not only the opposition between pure and impure but also the basic insights in the Hindu tradition: an eternal self, reincarnation, a meaningful place in this life that is determined by previous lives, the unity of all things in the divine.

38. Dietz-Sontheimer, "Die Ethik des Hinduismus," pp. 394-95. He points out that, for the rest, traditional Hindu society still rests on the foundations of family and caste. Cf. p. 422.

39. Ibid., p. 399.

40. C. van der Burg and P. van der Veen, "Ver van India, ver van Surinam: Hindoestaanse Surinamers in Nederland," in *Religieuze Bewegingen in Nederland* 12 (Amsterdam: VU Uitgeverij, 1986), pp. 29-30, indicate that caste opposition among Hindus — who entered the Netherlands via Surinam — has largely disappeared, apart from the consciousness of brahmanic origin.

41. S. K. Chatterji, "Some Aspects of Dalit Ideology," in *Religion and Society* 37 (1990): 11. A. M. Abraham Ayrookuzhiel, "The Ideological Nature of the Emerging Dalit Consciousness," *Religion and Society* 37 (1990): 16, indicates that the caste system continues in spite of reform under the influence of people such as Raja Rammohan Roy, Vivekananda, and Gandhi, as they do not touch the social and religious role of lower castes and their ritual hierarchy. Ayrookuzhiel suggests that even the membership in leftist unions in Kerala (where the communists came to power already in 1957) is determined by one's caste membership. "If a Dalit stands as party candidate for election, the Marxists who belong to non-dalit castes do not vote for him" (p. 19).

This discussion of duties within the caste system, however, falls far short of exhausting all there is to say about Hindu culture — there are other lines as well. During the expansive and long-lasting religious festivals the social hierarchy is broken and sometimes even turned around. In the bhakti movement the caste boundaries are often transcended.[42] The festivals also have a strong social function. M. Von Brück indicates that people of other belief systems, such as Christians, can also take part in the village festivals.[43] And there are also the *samnyasins,* who break away from ordered society and seek emancipation from the chain of the cycle of reincarnation by achieving union with the brahman. For the three higher castes the ideal, after they have performed their social duties, is to break away from their bonds in order to strive for emancipation from earthly existence.[44] This can be done in many ways: by withdrawing to lonely places, traveling, or even living in an *ashrama.* This consecration of life consists of the practice of virtue, thus involving morality as well. These ideal virtues have permeated Indian society. Whereas *duties* are derived from the dharma, the *virtues* for which one strives come from the higher religious values of the *samnyasins.*[45] The idea of *sattva* (ritual purity) finds expression in purity, justice, and integrity. The virtues that must be nourished are sympathy with all living creatures, patience, contentment, purity, tenderness, pure thoughts, and freedom from irritableness, jealousy, and malice.[46] The *samnyasin* and brahminic ideals of unselfishness and nonviolence (as well as the vegetarianism that accompanies them) influence society as a whole. They offer a continual point of departure for critique on society and social reforms.[47]

42. Van den Bosch, *Levende godsdiensten,* pp. 138, 70; Dietz-Sontheimer, "Die Ethik des Hinduismus," p. 411; as with the Sikhs, the caste boundaries are relative; see G. Dietz-Sontheimer, "Sikhs," in *Lexikon der Religionen* (Freiburg: Herder, 1987), p. 612.

43. Von Brück, "Sharing Religious Experience in Hindu-Christian Encounter," in *Sharing Religious Experience,* p. 145.

44. D. C. Mulder, "Het hindoeïsme," in *Antwoord,* ed. Sperna Weiland (Amsterdam: Meulenhoff, 1982), p. 55.

45. Dietz-Sontheimer, "Die Ethik des Hinduismus," p. 403; cf. Dumont, *Homo Hierarchicus,* pp. 184-87, 236.

46. Dietz-Sontheimer, "Die Ethik des Hinduismus," p. 410; cf. p. 417; he lists the classic texts on pp. 418-20.

47. Ibid., p. 395.

On the basis of the duties prescribed by the dharma and the ideals of purification and sanctification, one can understand the distinction between good and evil. All things are one; as we saw, this unity includes conflicting elements, but not everything is equally part of the divine. The loving attendant, the wise manager, and the purified guru realize the bond with the divine more than the robber and the thief. Everything is related to the actual but not in the same way, and therefore not everything is equally holy. This does not mean that all things are not interconnected. The fundamental aspect of humans is — whether one experiences it or not — the divine. If one realizes that the quietly incomprehensible, the eternal, immutable, colorless, and tasteless, without beginning and without end, lies at the basis of existence, then one is freed from death.[48] This is truly that: this reality, at its core, is that, the unformed, one, eternal, stilled brahman:

> These rivers, my dear, flow, the eastern toward the east, the western toward the west. They go just from the ocean to the ocean. They become the ocean itself. As there they know not "I am this one," "I am that one," — even so, indeed my dear, all creatures here, though they have come forth from Being, know not "We have come forth from Being." Whatever they are in this world, whether tiger, or lion, or wolf, or boar, or worm, or fly, or gnat, or mosquito, that they become.
>
> That which is the finest essence — this whole world has that as its self. That is Reality. That is *Atman*. That art thou, Śvetaketu.[49]

Reality is one: This is that. Order rules in reality and is reflected in rituals. Through rituals and duties life is placed within the framework of the cosmic whole.[50]

Viewed from the perspective of the prophetic traditions, the question arises as to how one distinguishes between good and evil. From the Jewish, Christian, and Muslim standpoint, the world is

---

48. Katha Upanishad 3.15.

49. Chandogya Upanishad 6.10.1-3, in *Source Book,* p. 69.

50. According to Gonda, *Religionen Indiens,* 1:293, for a long time sin was not personal moral guilt, but a violation of the world order; the objective guilt of the transgression is amended by the ceremony of reconciliation which removes the impurity.

separate from God and God acts in the world. According to the biblical conception, in this action God exercises partiality; he defends those who suffer unjustly and helps the poor. This separation between God and the world is simultaneously the condition for confirming the value of earthly life. Indeed, because the person is a creature, a created, finite existence belongs to the person. People neither know nor do everything; in the Bible this is not regarded as a disadvantage but rather as characteristic of human existence. People are not free if they retreat from the world to an immutable being beyond historical reality; they are free only if they live out of trust in God within historical reality. Within the relation between God and human beings, people have their own responsibility for their lives within society and nature. This responsibility also allows the possibility of wrong deeds,[51] which are seen not as violations of the cosmic order but as transgressions of God's law and violations of his intention for the world.

Within Hindu traditions salvation is indicated in the realization of the true Self, the unity with the divine or with the cosmic order: the dharma. As we saw, this allows for two variants: first, striving for unity with the brahman in emancipation from this world *(moksha)*; second, joining in the world order by meticulously fulfilling one's assigned tasks. Both are important for the possibility of prophetic critique of the existing social order.

If one strives for *moksha,* one stresses the maya character of the world. "Maya" means that the world is perceived as an independent entity, different from what it actually is, since it is only a manifestation of the one. People find salvation not in society but in their own *moksha* — emancipation from the bonds of illusion. This accounts for the presence of the *samnyasins.* As in traditional Christianity, the depreciation of "this world" in combination with a striving for personal salvation leads to avoidance of the world. Every person must go his or her own way — through many lives. Whoever views life in this way

---

51. Cf. the discussions on human responsibility and the possibility of doing evil; for example, A. Plantinga, "The Free Will Defence," in *The Philosophy of Religion,* ed. B. Mitchell (Oxford: Oxford University Press, 1971), pp. 105-20; V. Brümmer, "Moral Sensitivity and the Free Will Defence," *Neue Zeitschrift für systematische Theologie und Religionsphilosophie* 29 (1987): 86-100; A. van den Beld, "Kan de mens in het eeuwige leven niet meer zondigen?" in *Houdt het op met de dood?* ed. A. W. Messchenga and H. Vroom (Kampen: Kok, 1989), pp. 81-99.

calls others to turn from the corrupt world, which is the path that Hindu mystics take. This orientation toward actual emancipation can also take another turn, as it did with Gandhi. Then the contrast between truth and salvation on the one hand and actual society on the other provides the opportunity for a radical critique of the existing society and suggestions for improvement, such as Gandhi's critique of the treatment of the untouchables. Thus detachment from this world is the forerunner of prophetic critique. Emphasis on detachment and mysticism once provided the critical potential for criticizing the burning of widows.[52]

Conversely, should one emphasize the dharma, then one must designate part of the world as good and immutable. This part can be found especially in the dharma, the order of the world, and thus the rites prescribed in the Vedic writings receive an important place. If one considers the world order as divine, it is then difficult to find a point outside the order of society from which it can be criticized. It is difficult to understand how one can arrive at a prophetic critique from within popular Hindu religion and the traditional ritual religion.

When Western Christian theologians become acquainted with the Hindu writings — the Bhagavad Gita, the Mahabharata, the Puranas, the Upanishads — and see documentaries about lavish Hindu festivals, they are impressed by the integrity and depth of Hindu thought and also by the joy and thankfulness present in the popular religion. Many people have family altars, some examples of which can also be viewed in museums. By performing one's own duties, one is included in the great whole of reality in a meaningful way. The relativization of the distinction between life and death through belief in reincarnation makes the altruistic performance of duties possible. After all, everything is part of a great whole. Western concepts like equality, which are elaborated in equal rights, equal opportunity, equal access to food, education, and culture, stand in

52. See V. van Bijlert, "Raja Rammohun Roy's Thought and Its Relevance for Human Rights," in *Human Rights and Religious Values,* pp. 93-108. Because of Gandhi, inspiration for this is sometimes indicated as stemming from the gospel, but it does not seem fair to trace all critical voices in India back to Western influences. There is a particular obviousness to morality; see my "God and Goodness," in *Christian Faith and Philosophical Theology: Essays in Honour of Vincent Brümmer,* ed. G. van den Brink et al. (Kampen: Kok Pharos, 1992), pp. 250-57; here the Reformed tradition would speak of common grace.

another light because of this. On the one hand, there is solidarity with people and living creatures who are all part of the great whole and who during many lives try to find their way in existence. But on the other hand, the coupling of the hierarchy of the caste system with reincarnation offers the possibility of seeing one person as further ahead on the path of life and another as less advanced. In this way differences in opportunities and abilities can be transformed into a meaningful and *just* order determined by karma. Things are different in every successive life, but they are always meaningful and just.

When reality is viewed as a coherent, ordered, and meaningful system, everything must have its own place. Should the whole of reality emanate from a divine principle, then evil also has a place, so that it too becomes more or less meaningful. A distinction will ultimately be made between pleasant and unpleasant and between better and worse behavior, but in principle, good and evil, pleasant and unpleasant, just and unjust actions, life and death — all exist in one great cohesion. They have their place within the great cosmic order. The Bhagavad Gita words it quite impressively:

> Understanding *(buddhi)*, knowledge *(jnâna)*, freedom from bewilderment, patience, truth, self-control and calmness; pleasure and pain, existence and non-existence, fear and fearlessness. Non-violence, equal-mindedness, contentment, austerity, charity, fame and ill-fame, the different states of beings proceed from Me alone.[53]

All the diversity of human existence emanates from the Lord Krishna: the good and the bad days, sexuality and birth as well as strict celibacy, success as well as failure, life as well as death. Everything emanates from the divine energy and returns to it. Everything has a place. Yet does this not declare the dissimilar — life and death, just and unjust, joy and grief, happiness and sadness — to be similar? Of course Hindus know what feasts and cremations are, what is better and what is worse, but, because the whole is viewed *holistically*, all things — adverse things included — are placed within a meaningful cohesion. The criterion for seeing things positively or negatively lies in the dharma (not, for example, in the "pursuit of happiness,"[54] the human striving

53. Bhagavad Gita 10.4-5, in *Source Book,* p. 135.
54. The American Bill of Rights, 1776, in *Boodschap uit de stilte: mysterie als*

for maximal happiness for the maximal number of people). A person has his or her legitimate and appointed place in the whole of things when he or she merges into the dharma. In addition, a person's self is, at bottom, divine; the core of a person remains untouched by suffering and dying. The actual Self is unaffected, eternal, and blessed. But within this religious philosophy of life how does one deal with poverty and injustice, with the untouchables and the wealthy? However much one is impressed by the depth of Hindu thought and literature and however much one respects the multiplicity of life, from the Christian point of view, one cannot evade the question of the boundary between good and evil in this world — a boundary that cannot be allowed to deteriorate and cannot be allowed to be associated primarily with the observation of rites and the fulfillment of duties that belong to one's caste.

These questions are directly related to the concept of God. Not all Hindus believe in God. Some schools have an impersonal concept of the all-encompassing whole and observe those rites that are in harmony with the cosmic order. Other Hindus do believe in God and worship God in a specific manner, as Vishnu, Shiva, Durga, or something else. The worship of a personal God (bhakti) is the most common form of religion in India. Within Vaishnavism God is regarded as a person and a creator, but God is also both all that exists and the source of all that exists — both the emanations and the source of emanations.[55] One strives to attain unity with God, strives for

openbaring, ed. J. van Baal (Baarn: Ten Have, 1991), p. 111; cf. L. Swidler, "Human Rights: A Historical Overview," in The Ethics of World Religions and Human Rights, Concilium 1990, no. 2 (London: SCM; Philadelphia: Trinity Press International, 1990), pp. 16-17.

55. H. Keilman, "Het Godsbeeld in de Vaisnava Filosofie," in Godsbeelden in verschillende religieuze tradities, ed. W. Haan (Amsterdam: VU Uitgeverij, 1985), p. 58. See also Ramanuja himself: The Vedanta Sutras with the Commentary by Ramanuja, tr. G. Thibaut (Oxford, 1904; reprint Delhi: Motilal Banarsidass, 1984), p. 131: absolute unity implies ignorance (and ignorance, evil), and thus "you are that" may not be explained [as in the Advaita Vedanta] as an undifferentiated unity, but is present in the absolute distinction [and is the omniscient brahman]. Because the brahman is differentiated, the world is his body ("the entire aggregate of things, intelligent and non-intelligent, has its Self in Brahman in so far as it constitutes Brahman's body," p. 134) and the divine can be represented as a person (p. 488, with the result that the question of why the creation came to be is also discussed, pp. 486-87).

complete fulfillment in existence by becoming one with the primal source. Within the bhakti movement, this unity is achieved by surrendering in faith, through which one finally achieves complete unity with God.[56] The idea of unity remains fundamental. The bhakti movement worships a God who is perceived as a person. The divinity is highly exalted, lord of the world, infinite and immutable, the eternal seed of all creatures, just and impartial. Vishnu has come to the aid of people in earthly forms *(avataras),* the best known of which are Rama and Krishna. On the one hand, they come to help people restore the world order; on the other, they are manifestations of the One.[57] Thus the bhakti movement has a personal concept of God and a personal relation with God even though at the same time God is the deeper unity of all things.

The Advaita Vedanta rejects the idea of a personal God; according to this school, the supreme, the divine, the ground of all that exists, must be regarded as impersonal. But here too, the characteristic *satcitananda* (true, blessed, and loving) is attributed to the brahman.[58] Because of pantheism or panentheism, God is not an absolute "opposite." The holistic conception of the world leaves no room for God or a norm that stands in opposition to the world and that acts as an "opposition" party in history. The divine is everything; the norm is the cosmic order that permeates and sustains things. Because life and death, success and failure are part of one organic whole, the distinction between good and evil fades, and the religious leader is not a prophet but a pandit or a guru. The religious leader is not someone who reveals a way of life and justice but someone who performs the rites (pandit) or reveals the way to unity with the divine (guru). Judaism and Christianity hold that humans are created in the image of God, but

---

56. Keilman, "Het Godsbeeld in de Vaisnava Filosofie," p. 61; Gonda, *Religionen Indiens,* 1:244.

57. Gonda, *Religionen Indiens,* 1:250. I will not give a detailed comparison of the *avataras* and incarnation. Similarity exists in the salvific will of God and difference in the scope of the love of Krishna and Jesus (believers, and believers but also enemies, respectively), the evil from which one is freed (ignorance, karma, and reincarnation; and blindness, sin, and death, respectively); Christ is not God in the form of a man but a real man; see R. DeSmet, "Jesus and the Avatara," in *Dialogue and Syncretism,* ed. J. D. Gort et al. (Grand Rapids: Eerdmans; Amsterdam: Rodopi, 1989), pp. 153-62. Christology is discussed in ch. 4; what is said there obtains here a fortiori.

58. See my *Religions and the Truth,* pp. 124-25.

not that they are one with God. Judaism and Christianity also have reservations about denoting the divine by sexual symbols — the union of the *yoni* and the *linga* — not to mention worshiping these symbols. An image of the goddess or god with a head that emerges from the *linga* is inconceivable within the three Semitic religions. These symbols must be interpreted carefully in order to do justice to the meaning they hold for Hindus. Diana Eck reports how early Western travelers in India were appalled by these sexual symbols. She cautions against exaggerating the sexual background of the religious symbol:[59] it refers to the unity of all things within the divine. But even if one is aware of this background, the fact remains that the divine energy produces and sustains all things and therefore is *not in* all things but *is itself* the supporting basis of and in all things. This is a monistic philosophy: *everything* is of divine origin.

The first question that arises from Christianity with respect to the Hindu religions concerns the standard for good and evil: for biblical religions, the pressing question is why people are not equally seen as images of God. A second question concerns the value of enjoying daily life. Are not rituals and the maintenance of the dharma emphasized too much on the one hand and detachment from the world (in the *samnyasins*) on the other? There is also the question of the concept of God: Is the deep experience of God — to which many Hindu writings attest — an experience of union with God, or is it an experience of the nearness of and alliance with God, who is a partner of people, and therefore should not be understood as the deepest ground *in and of* existence but, rather, as distinguished from it? It is difficult to see how great Hindu traditions can really conceive of God as a person: how can one think that God is the deeper unity of all that exists, and then continue to hold to the ideas of the cosmic order and karma? I will make two more comments on this. First, it remains to be seen what Hindus in the bhakti movement actually believe, particularly whether the idea of the cosmic order has receded into the background for many, and whether the unity with the divine is experienced and understood more as a relation than as a union of being.

59. Eck, *Banaras,* pp. 103-6. Pictures of such images can be found in Zimmer, *Myths and Symbols,* ill. 64; J. Ayers, *Die Kunst Asiens,* Catalogus Victoria and Albert Museum, London, III (London: Scala/Philip Wilson; Munich: Beck, 1983), p. 60. In Eck, *Banaras,* p. 104, a *linga* with five faces is portrayed.

Second, in further elaborating on God's being as a person, I would qualify this notion in ways that I cannot pursue within the framework of this book.

3.4 Reincarnation and *Moksha*

The doctrines discussed above — the union of all that exists in brahman, the dharma that sustains all things — are systematically connected to the belief in reincarnation. The union, with one or two exceptions, is not realized in this life but later. Given the disorder that one sees, the world order is not realized now but only through many lives: karma ensures that one reaps what one sows. In this way the distinction between that which is real *(sat)* and ordered on the one hand and that which is not (real) and without order on the other is connected to the ideas of reincarnation and karma. Reincarnation is also connected to belief in brahman; the belief that people are part of the great process of all that exists and that they in their essence are one with the divine, brings with it the idea that they are "indestructible." They have always been and always will be. Only their circumstances change, with each life different from the one before. In the end they will be emancipated and merge with brahman. Thus human beings could be divided into at least two parts: a temporal part and an eternal part, the physical and the soul, which is connected to the divine.[60] In their concrete life people are limited by "name and form," by the concreteness of existence. The physical aspect of human beings is the car that the soul drives.

Given this view of the person, it is clear that the atman is reincarnated. Or at least, as a silent witness, the self always remains unaltered.[61] R. Kranenborg describes reincarnation as the conviction

---

60. One should actually distinguish (at least) three parts in a person: the physical, the consciousness in this life, and the eternal that is reincarnated, carries the karma, and is one with the brahmin. Cf. Satprakashananda, *Methods of Knowledge* (London: Allen and Unwin, 1965), p. 45. One thinks of the individual "I" that thinks but about which one cannot think without it becoming an object (me): I think about me (myself). But what is that I?

61. Radhakrishnan, *An Idealist View of Life* (1932; reprint London: Unwin, 1980), p. 162.

"that there is something in the person that in one way or another returns to this earth after death again (and that, consequently, was already on this earth before birth)."[62] Thus the identity of a person through a series of lives lies in the atman.[63] Because the atman passes from one life to another, the atman must have built up a quality that determines the next life. This determining factor is karma, which is the result of good and evil deeds in former lives. Every life contributes to karma and karma determines the reincarnation of the atman. In a subsequent life one pays for the wrongs one has done or reaps rewards for the good. A chance is given to find out what is required and to develop oneself further. Reincarnation is not restricted to people but obtains for all living creatures, including inanimate objects.

Because good and bad deeds are determinative for a successive life, there have been attempts to establish the specific consequences of immoral deeds, making lists of sins and their consequences. According to one such list, coveting the possessions of others and evil thoughts lead to birth in a low caste. Abusing others, lying, and gossiping cause one to return in the form of an animal or bird. Stealing, wounding people, and adultery cause one to become an inanimate object.[64] In this way everyone receives what she or he merits — a system viewed as just, for otherwise the attainment of ultimate salvation would be a question of chance.[65] Because it is so difficult to avoid all wrongs, it is not easy to secure a good rebirth, and therefore it is understandable that the cycle of rebirth is long. It concerns a laborious purification, a long process of perfection, including being set back if one falls into sin because of weakness. One must count on many, many lives, many difficulties, and many processes of dying.

As we have seen, the caste system is interwoven with this doctrine of merit. Being born into a low caste is better than being born as an animal, but of course a birth in a high caste is even better. The

---

62. R. Kranenborg, *Reïncarnatie en Christelijk Geloof* (Kampen: Kok, 1989), p. 25.

63. I will not deal here with questions relating to the possibility of the human identity in the atman, detached from concrete life. These questions are also important with respect to belief in the resurrection of the dead. See Kranenborg, *Reïncarnatie,* pp. 118-19; J. Hick, *Death and Eternal Life* (New York: Harper & Row, 1976), pp. 278-96.

64. Van den Bosch, *Levende godsdiensten,* p. 120.

65. P. Bowes, *The Hindu Religious Tradition* (London: Routledge and Kegan Paul, 1977), p. 56.

caste system is part of the cosmic order of the world. The rights and duties are set, but they are not determinative for someone's entire existence, simply for this life. If one lives a good life, then one moves to a higher caste. One's caste is determined by the karma one has built up oneself.[66] In addition, modern Hindu philosophers often hold that the caste system does indeed belong to the Indian culture, but not perforce to Hindu traditions. The caste system is said to have developed when the Aryans entered India, after which a particular societal gradation developed that was apparently integrated into the religious body of ideas.[67] In fact, it is not a necessary element of religion that is at issue here but rather a social stratification of Indian culture.

But whether the caste system is a characteristic feature of the Hindu tradition is beside the point. If the rigid caste system — including the burning of widows and the neglect of girls — would disappear entirely, then it would obtain that (a) a person's starting situation in life is determined by his or her own karma, (b) the troubles encountered in life are a means to develop a better karma, and (c) a person's prosperity rests not only on chance but also on her or his earlier rewards. The ideas of karma and reincarnation are not necessarily linked to the caste system, but they are related to differences in status and situation. This problem would not be solved if the caste system would become less rigid or even disappear in time. In assessing the ideas of karma and reincarnation from the perspective of the prophetic traditions, one can only say that social criticism has

66. J. C. Heesterman, "Caste and Karma: Max Weber's Analysis of Caste," in *Inner Conflict of Tradition,* pp. 194-202, qualifies Weber's characterization of the connection of karma and caste as "the most consistent theodicy ever produced" and "caste soteriology" (p. 195). In his opinion, there is an enormous tension here because karma determines the fate of the few, but caste and the *svadharma* (the duties of the caste) make the person subordinate to a collective. Because there are always things that go wrong in society, one cannot break through one's karma unless one steps out of the collective system. Thus the doctrine of karma breaks out of the collective world of dharma in the direction of individual salvation, ultimately threatening the order of society. This is the reason, writes Heesterman, for the quiet resistance to renunciation (p. 199). Cf. also his view on the dynamics in the relation between the *varnas* and the *jatis* (castes), pp. 199-200.

67. For example, Bowes, *Hindu Religious Tradition,* p. 7. Beginning already in the last century, reform movements, e.g., the Brahma Samaj, have tried to breach the caste system. See P. Antes, "Das neue im modernen Hinduismus," *Zeitschrift für Missiologie und Religionswissenschaft* 57 (1973): 104-5.

little chance here. The doctrine of reincarnation gives plenty of opportunity for sanctioning social and economic inequality, but it is difficult to see how prophets and social innovators will ever be given an opportunity in a tradition that explains the destiny of people in terms of karma and reincarnation.

This difficulty can be clearly seen if I introduce a Western expression at this point that is determinative for humanist, Christian, and socialist ideals: a "just society." From the perspective of a worldview that assumes that people live in this world only once, the range within which "justice" must be realized falls within this life: the child that dies of hunger is dead and will not return. "Justice" is a task that needs to be fulfilled here and now. But from the viewpoint of karma and reincarnation, "justice" is not simply a concern for today: justice is played out in the entire cycle of reincarnations, in samsara. A person's point of departure is arranged justly and well. Thus one worldview differs from another with respect to what people regard as just and how they give content to the idea of justice. Its meaning is determined by the fabric of all the fundamental insights of a worldview.[68] For worldviews that take only physical life into account, "justice" concerns the historical situation in which people live; it is directed toward the distribution of resources in the world and not the justice of the karmic structure of the succession of reincarnations. In the one case, "giving to each his or her due" is directed toward those living at the time; in the other case, it is directed toward the karmic law that provides the proper reincarnation for everything throughout the whole of reality.

The way of escape from the cycle of reincarnation lies in *moksha*, emancipation from karma, which can be achieved by stillness and detachment. The remark made above on the context of the meaning of the concept of justice within the whole of a worldview can also be applied to the concept of emancipation. Emancipation here is not directed toward the emancipation from oppressors as in the Enlightenment tradition after the French Revolution and in the socialist tradition after the Communist Manifesto. Emancipation from the bonds of karma does not concern political emancipation but detachment from the karmic history. It is often said — not without reason — that all religions concern salvation and emancipation. However, the ideas of "salvation" and "emancipation" clearly differ. Emancipation

68. Cf. my *Religions and the Truth*, ch. 10.

74

from karma is closer to the Christian idea of emancipation from the guilt of sin than to political emancipation. In Christian belief the goal of emancipation from sin is twofold: (a) to be able to live properly in this broken world, (b) sharing in the resurrection of the dead. The goal of emancipation of karma is a return of the individual Self to the divine — an objective that agrees more with the second Christian objective than with the first. The Hindu religion concurs with the first Christian objective — in short, living properly — that people must try to do their duty and to live properly in order to achieve good karma or even to escape karma. Thus one reads in the Bhagavad Gita:

> 6. Desire and hatred, pleasure and pain, the aggregate [the organism], intelligence, and steadfastness described — this in brief is the field along with its modifications.
> 7. Humility [absence of pride], integrity [absence of deceit], non-violence, patience, uprightness, service of the teacher, purity of body and mind, steadfastness, and self-control,
> 8. Indifference to the objects of sense, self-effacement, and the perception of the evil of birth, death, old age, sickness, and pain . . .
> 11. This is declared to be true knowledge, and all that is different from it is non-knowledge.[69]

This passage concerns high ideals and resolve, wise people filled with compassion. It is worth noting that not only are there significant resemblances to Christian virtues but also fundamental differences. This is often the case when one compares worldviews: seldom are they in opposition with each other, they have much in common, and, aside from their fundamental differences, in many areas they overlap.[70] In comparing the two and weighing them against each other, one must keep in mind the context in which these ideals are articulated. As the passage quoted above continues, the differences with the Christian beliefs appear:

> 9. Non-attachment, absence of clinging to son, wife, home, and the like, and a constant equal-mindedness to all desirable and undesirable happenings,

69. Excerpts from Bhagavad Gita 13.6-11, in *Source Book,* p. 146.
70. I detail this in my *Religions and the Truth,* ch. 12.

10. Unswerving devotion to Me with wholehearted discipline, resort to solitary places, dislike for a crowd of people,
11. Constancy in the knowledge of the Spirit, insight into the end of the knowledge of Truth — this is declared to be true knowledge, and all that is different from it is non-knowledge.[71]

Christians feel that attachment to their wives, children, and friends is good. Unselfish attachment is an obvious ideal for people who love and care about each other. Within the Semitic religions, indifference to a life of companionship is not usually regarded as wise. The love of solitude is useful for repentance, but it is not an ideal way of life (at least not in the Protestant Christian traditions). Wild orgies and excessive pleasure are to be avoided, but good companionship is esteemed highly. This is unlike the ideal of *moksha*. Both the Bhagavad Gita and the apostle Paul argue for self-control. The Bhagavad Gita believes self-control goes hand in hand with an internal or even external distancing from society, whereas for Paul self-control is practiced in the midst of many people, but it is not self-control as indifference to all companionship. He holds himself apart from this world because it manifests irredeemable evils, yet his internal distance does not involve social life as such, but only that which is wrong in this order of existence. Although much is lacking in this world and the order of this world is passing away, Paul still expects a changed and improved world, not emancipation from this world as such.[72]

Many traditional Hindu moral values coincide with Christian virtues, yet the context in which they are concretized differs. Thus the import of concepts such as emancipation and detachment changes; different beliefs lead to different ways of experiencing reality. One must take into account that a religious tradition goes through significant developments and that people become familiar with religious texts in various ways. In the past the church also viewed marriage and sexuality with suspicion; the Roman Catholic Church still forbids priests to marry. But many Christians, Protestant as well as Roman Catholic, believe that sexuality has a legitimate place within lasting relationships.

Similar differences between official and actual belief naturally

71. Bhagavad Gita 13.9-11, in *Source Book,* p. 146.
72. See 1 Cor. 7:31; 15:40-49.

76

exist in the Hindu tradition as well. Through the variety of schools in the Hindu world — the movements of austerity and salvation, the festivals and the surrender to belief, the ritual ceremonies — one is able to apply different aspects of life in its diverse phases to other parts of the tradition. Not everything is always real; not everything that is done is equally important in the actual experience of belief. As a matter of fact, most people aspire to live well for the purpose of being reincarnated in a good manner without striving for *moksha*. Actual belief for the most part concerns *this* life, to survive and to achieve some measure of fulfillment. One is reminded of the three levels of religiosity that I have already mentioned: (a) religious acts that are directed toward survival and the improvement of the conditions of life, (b) efforts that are directed toward the acquisition of rewards and a good reincarnation, and (c) efforts that are directed toward emancipation and the realization of the eternal self. From the point of view of those Christian traditions that have no monks or nuns, there is much to be said for this first form of religiosity. Religion that deals with the issues of this life is closer to many Christian traditions than religion that is directed toward detachment from this reality. It could therefore be said that Hindus and Christians living in the same street need not differ in their behavior and the practice of their belief as much as one might expect by comparing their theological-philosophical doctrines. In practice, honesty and reliability without the presence of jealousy and greed are important.

From within a Christian point of view the question remains as to how the good life is achieved within the Hindu belief. From within Protestant theology one must ask how a person becomes good and just. Is it by doing good works? Does one gather karma for a good reincarnation? Does upholding the rites, dharma, or regulations of the law make one good and just? The Hindu evaluation that several lives are needed if one is to learn anything and "improve" oneself seems realistic: a person cannot possibly learn enough in one life, as he or she is quite limited. In addition, people are held responsible for their deeds; everyone must make an effort.

Countering this, however, is the argument that goodness is not a stable characteristic that can be acquired. People who are very good can change completely after a few bad years. Friendly people can commit war crimes. Humans are apparently such that, if under pressure long enough and detached from the people they love, they are capable of doing anything. There are no exceptions. Thus the struggle to better oneself through a long series of lives could prove to be endless. Hindu acknowledgment as to the weight and duration of this method is realistic — there is no optimistic Western belief in progress here. Yet technological progress and higher standards of living surely do not necessarily imply that people themselves have improved. One cannot say that there is continuous moral improvement through the course of time.[73] Can people really perfect themselves and be freed from sin?

Many people recognize that this is impossible and pray to the gods for mercy. But if in important traditions in India one is dependent on grace, then how can one hold to a unity of the divine and the human? If one is compelled to acknowledge the fragility and fallibility of people, so that grace is necessary, then surely one cannot believe that people are ultimately divine and that the cosmic order of the world is good? It is the pronouncement of existence — the cosmic order, usually including the hierarchy of ranks and castes — as good that leads to resignation to injustice. If nature is professed to be holy, why build dams or fight cancer? After all, things are the way they should be! The reverse of this is that Western society, which sometimes creates the impression of wanting to experience everything in one life, can kindle dissatisfaction because that dream does not become reality. As mentioned in the preceding chapter, Abe believes that emphasis on justice leads to strife. In this chapter I noted that Biardeau suggests that Western individualism is at odds with Hindu tradition. The negative consequences of Western individualism are immense. It used to be said, "Each for oneself and God for us all"; but, since many no longer believe in God, it has become "Each for oneself and nobody for all." People have, want, and use too much, to such a degree that nature is threatened and others in the world do not have enough. Paying attention to the order of nature, awareness of the secret of

---

73. When the Iron Curtain fell and the Berlin Wall was demolished in 1989, the East European states achieved freedom from communist oppression. Havel was elected in Prague, while Gorbachev and Yeltsin implemented changes in the Soviet Union. European history appeared to have taken a favorable turn. But within three years, due to deep conflicts, the East European states have disintegrated, innumerable war crimes have occurred in former Yugoslavia, and racism has increased tremendously in West European countries. The future looks bleak because evil does not go away. But who, after the Holocaust, really thought that technological advances would resolve the problem of evil?

creation, searching for a life that fits within the whole of that which exists — such aspects of religion are valuable. One must distinguish between maintaining dharma and respecting the balance of nature. A traditional religious doctrine of the cosmic order does not correspond with concern for nature.

There are, however, a few basic thoughts in the Hindu traditions that seem to have great significance for today: the person as part of society, priority given not to individual rights but to duties and re-sponsibilities, the person's connectedness with all things, and the divine mystery behind things. But because the divine, "real," and good lies in the things — permeates everything — and is not above or over against them, the normative character of that which is good and right threatens to fade, and the divine can be identified with that which already is, undermining the prophetic power of this tradition. The *samnyasin* can detach himself from society and present ideals of detach-ment and love, just as a long series of gurus do in their ashrams, but the way of salvation is finally a very personal one. What staying power can a prophetic critique of society, like that of Gandhi, have?

Belief in reincarnation is ultimately a question of fact: either it occurs or it does not. Because belief in reincarnation and social criti-cism are at odds, it is essential for people who believe in reincarnation to defend their belief. Since belief in reincarnation can have a great effect on other people, it is not enough simply to say that this belief needs no more proof than any other belief. Any belief that affects one's attitude toward others — and most beliefs do — must be defended in public discussion. Kranenborg has described the origin of belief in reincarnation and given a summary of the objections to it.[74] I will mention a few objections to belief in reincarnation as present in the Hindu tradition.

74. Kranenborg, *Reïncarnatie,* pp. 30-92, 139-46. On the false allegation that belief in reincarnation had a place in the early Christian church, cf. R. Roukema, "Reïncarnatie in de oude kerk," *Gereformeerd Theologisch Tijdschrift* 92 (1992): 199-218; 93 (1993): 33-56. It was always condemned. Reincarnation does not appear even in Origen; he rejects the notion as being in conflict with the gospel (pp. 36-37); his idea of other lives in other worlds is more a "solution" for the problem of the freedom and finitude of a person in the hereafter (and certainly not a result of karma); see pp. 215-18, 39-40. On the problem of human freedom and responsibility in the hereafter, cf. A. van den Beld, "Kan de mens in het eeuwig leven niet meer zondigen?" in *Houdt het op met de dood?* pp. 81-99.

First, I do not believe that all things (people, animals, trees, plants, and possibly stones) have a permanent, immutable "self" that takes first one and then another "name and form" — a divine Self that is reincarnated in the mouse and the lily, the spider and the sundew, the tiger and the oak tree, the poor and the rich.

Second, I do not see how one atman can exist through an endless cycle of reincarnations as person, animal, or plant. What makes him or her "the same"?

Third, I fail to see the meaningful order shown by the endless series of forms of existence. One can refer to the karmic laws in order to comprehend this order, but is not someone required to enforce the laws? I do not have a clear grasp of the karmic bookkeeping system. Who keeps the account up-to-date? What is the rationality within this karmic system? How is a curse weighed against a blessing? If someone is beaten repeatedly, is that compensation for sins and an opportunity to learn? Some people have done a poorer job with their former life than others and the debts of that former life are put on their account! The villain has only himself to blame; he can hope for the willingness and love of others but has no right to expect it. The karmic system requires a rationality in the world order and, especially in modern Western ideas of reincarnation, a progressive development in history. Such a progression is problematic in view of the great historical disasters. The genocide of the Jews in the Second World War shocked many.[75] If one takes seriously the Holocaust, which occurred in one of the most "developed" countries, then the belief that people learn something new in each life and that life gets better each time seems very naive.

Some Christian and Muslim views hold that misfortune arises through divine ordination. That is a harsh belief: would God really want that? Why does the one person suffer misfortunes and not the other? Yet the combination of karma and reincarnation implies that people who have suffered much have only themselves to blame, or must attempt to become wiser, which seems even harsher. Unfortunately, effort and good intentions do not always have the intended effect. I do not see the order of the world in this way. The righteous often fare badly, which seems to argue against the notion of a good

---

75. See, for example, E. L. Fackenheim, *God's Presence in History* (New York and London: Harper Torch Books, 1972), pp. 84ff.; as well as idem, *The Jewish Return into History* (New York: Schocken, 1978), passim.

karmic order. The Christian (and Jewish) view of the suffering of the righteous seems more profound and more in accord with reality than the conjecture that what goes wrong here is, as seen from a higher (karmic) plan, *just* and *meaningful*. At this point I would like to remind the reader of how the Buddhist Abe with his Zen background allowed the distinction between good and evil on the one hand (in the normal life, samsara) to stand, but from the "higher" plane *(shunyata)* regarded it as relative. It rains on the good and evil alike. It is an experiential truth that the just and legitimate course of affairs is often thwarted by all sorts of things. This empirical wisdom argues against a theory of justice on a higher plane, karma, that causes good or evil to arise in frameworks beyond our comprehension and view — our former and future lives.[76] Things are just not that straightforward. Evil is understood to be justice here; trouble is given a legitimate place in our lives. If I had to choose between this Hindu teaching and the Buddhist view, then the latter, however sadder and wiser, would nonetheless appear more plausible. It is necessary to relativize human achievements, as already seen in chapter two. I would like to introduce this relativization as an objection to the doctrine of karma, and in chapter four I return to this in another context.

Fourth, the serious social consequences of such a view — people do not suffer for nothing! — has nothing to do with the weakness of the proofs for reincarnation. On the grounds of the enormous implications for practical life, one may demand that belief in reincarnation be defended more adequately before conclusions are drawn. Stories of "memories of former lives" — as a person, animal, or tree? — can sometimes be explained by means other than reincarnation, which sometimes give one cause to think. There is more to this world than meets the eye. But that is not to say that the doctrine of almost endless reincarnation is plausible — the evidence is very weak and the objections are strong. A skeptical attitude is appropriate.

We thus come to the end of this discussion of several beliefs in the Hindu tradition. I first examined the idea that all things at bottom

---

76. The Bible also speaks about human lack of understanding of events; see Isa. 55:8; Amos 3:6. See also Job's wrestling with misery, which ends in his acknowledgment of God's greatness (Job 40:3ff.). But God's involvement with the world is not karmatic. For the Christian understanding of evil, Jesus' word in John 9:3-4 is central.

are connected to or even are one with the primal source of everything that exists: the brahman. People come into contact with this mysterious fundamental reality in many ways. The presence of many stories illustrate how bewildering, confusing, and impressive reality is. As the main objection to the holistic (and pan[en]theistic) view on reality, I have posited that, if everything at bottom is divine, good is associated with the cosmic order so that there is a place for ritualism, the caste system can be included within the necessary order of things, and one's duty must be placed above virtues such as mercy and solidarity. We then saw that a holistic view can easily be linked with the doctrine of reincarnation. After all, if all things are expressions of the one reality, then in a certain sense they are eternal and immutable. In other words, there is a connection of being between all things; all things share in the same being or self. With regard to Hindu ideals concerning the way of life — simplicity, righteousness, and so on — I have expressed respect and a sensitivity to this connectedness.

But I have also brought objections to the doctrine of reincarnation. In addition to intellectual objections on the basis of the question of human individuality and the working of karma, I find it implausible that differences in happiness and unhappiness, prosperity and poverty, spiritual power and weakness between people should rest on the karma they have built up in former lives. I then posited that a faith with important implications for social life must give an account of itself. In addition to these critical notions I also indicated valuable elements: emphasis on the existence of a person within the community and on the responsibilities that one has, implicit or explicit criticism on attachment and possessions in the *samnyasin* movement, and attention to internalization, contemplation, and sanctification. Can one be anything but impressed by the Bhagavad Gita when it says that one must complete one's task because it is a task and not because it ensures success and personal happiness? At the same time, however, one must still raise the question as to what someone's task consists in. If it does not lie in the cosmic order, dharma, then where does it lie? And if the divine does not permeate all things — in all their ambiguities — but is independent of creation, how does one then speak of God? These last questions mark the transition to the monotheistic religions, which acknowledge God's independence from creation. Chapter four focuses on Islam.

4

The One God, the Prophet, and the Cross

4.1 Introduction

The previous chapter ended with a distinction between God and the world. In contrast to the Hindu notion that human beings are fundamentally, at the core of their being, related to all things, even to the divine that supports and permeates all things, I introduced the idea that the difference between good and evil implies that all things are not at bottom divine, since they can be good as well as evil. God is to be distinguished from the evil in the world, whereas in the world good and evil are intermingled. In prophetic religions God is viewed as the Creator and therefore as distinct from the world. God is with the world, but the world is not divine; on the one hand God is exalted above the world, while, on the other, he is near to it.

Central to Islam is its confession of God as Creator and the only God: "God is Unique! God is the Source [for everything]; He has not fathered anyone nor was He fathered, and there is nothing comparable to Him!"[1] *Islam* means "surrender in faith": Muslims trust in God, who guides the lives of humans. As Sir Muhammad Iqbal said, it is love for God that permeates all of life,[2] and by this love is meant concrete faith, faith-knowledge in action. I will use the term *islam*

---

1. From sura 112. All Koranic texts are cited from *The Qur'an,* tr. and commentary by T. B. Irving (Al-Hajj Ta'lim 'Ali) (Brattleboro, Vt.: Amana, 1985).
2. In A. Schimmel, *Gabriel's Wing: A Study into the Religious Ideas of Sir Muhammed Iqbal* (Leiden: Brill, 1963), p. 28. Hussein Masr, *Sufi Essays* (London: Allen and Unwin, 1972), pp. 146ff., writes that the inner unity of religions lies in this practical knowledge of faith.

(italicized, lower case) to refer to this surrendering in faith. Its normal capitalized form, "Islam," however, denotes the religious tradition. Naturally, a religious tradition as broad as Islam includes different accents. Those who are sympathetic to the more experiential, mystical school in Islam, the sufis, emphasize the love for God and people as the cornerstone of religion. For other Muslims the accent may lie more on obedience: *islam* as obedience in faith. But then it also involves *islam* in trusting in the providence and graciousness of God. Islam has been portrayed in the West as a legalistic religion, but that is not its central core. Christianity also has legalistic schools, and Paul used "obedience" as a pregnant term for the act of faith as well.[3] The essence of Islam is the belief in the one God, maker of all things, who knows all things, will judge all deeds, and is also merciful.

From the perspective of the Western/European ideal of a neutral, pluriform state, it is remarkable that Islam attempts to bring the whole of life into submission to God's will. Faith does not concern a sector of life — no, the whole of life is *islam*. It is difficult to have a secularized part of life, removed from the surrender in faith, because faith concerns the whole life: there is only one reality. Islam rejects every dualism in the world (an area of faith over and above that of another part of life where faith has no influence).[4] Belief can never be a purely personal affair of which other people take no notice, because God is the maker of all people and of the whole world. There is no other beside God and therefore no other power may usurp that role in any area of life. Every division in life is rejected.

That faith envelops life can be seen in the five pillars of Islam: the profession of faith, prayers, *zakat* (the giving of alms), fasting during the month of Ramadan, and the pilgrimage to Mecca.[5] The profession of faith that marks a person as a Muslim reads: "I believe that there is no other god than God and that Muhammad is his

3. Phil. 2:12; see E. Lohmeyer, *Die Briefe an die Philipper, an die Kolosser und an Philemon* (Göttingen: Vandenhoeck & Ruprecht, 1964[13]), p. 101.

4. See S. M. Zaman, "Place of Man in the Universe in the World-View of Islam," *Islamic Studies* 25 (1986): 325, where he states that in order to determine the correct behavior, one must know the place of humans in the universe; service to God encompasses the whole of life. Such was the ideal of Iqbal, who helped form the ideals of the Pakistani state. On this latter point cf. Schimmel, *Gabriel's Wing*, p. 267.

5. For that which follows, see A. Wessels, *Inleiding in de islam,* Levende Godsdiensten 1/1 (Heerlen: Open Theologisch Onderwijs, 1990), pp. 51-61.

Prophet."[6] This testimony must not be understood merely in an intellectual way. It is not simply an external declaration that one accepts that there is one God. Rather, it involves the recognition that God is actually GOD, the one who is exalted above humans and whose command must be obeyed if salvation is to be obtained. Knowledge is still highly esteemed in Islam, as it is knowledge and insight that provide the key to proper actions.[7] The confession of one God has meaning for the whole of life. The worst sin is *shirk,* giving God "companions" — worshiping more gods. Because God is the only God, polytheism denotes a turning away from God and his will.[8]

The ritual prayers *(salat)* enclose the day, just as the divine offices in Christian monasteries do. A Muslim prays the *salat* five times a day; in addition, all important matters are accompanied by spontaneous prayers. The *salat* is connected to the rising and setting of the sun. Before the *salat* one purifies oneself according to an established ritual, which involves partial or full bathing, with the conscious intention of purifying oneself for God. From the minaret of the mosque the following call is sounded: "God is most great [immeasurably great]!" (repeated four times); "I testify that there is no god but God" (two times); "I testify that Muhammad is the Prophet of God" (two times); "Come to prayer" (two times); "Come to salvation" (two times); "Prayer is better than sleep" (two times at dawn); "God is most great" (two times); "There is no god but God."[9] In Islamic countries, Muslims usually gather in the mosque, where, after an introduction, they face Mecca and, standing, declare their intention to perform the *salat.* The first sura (chapter) of the Koran is cited and they bow, only to stand straight up again. The worshipers then kneel, placing the knees, hands, and forehead on the ground. This kneeling is repeated. With every transition between kneeling, standing, and bowing, they confess: "God is most great!" This cycle of worship is repeated a

6. J. Slomp and A. Karagül, "Anders Geloven," in *Wereldgodsdiensten in Nederland* (Amersfort: De Horstink, 1991), p. 30.

7. F. Rosenthal, *Knowledge Triumphant* (Leiden: Brill, 1970), pp. 247-48.

8. W. Montgomery Watt, *Bells Inleiding tot de Koran,* tr. N. J. G. Kaptein (Utrecht: De Ploeg, 1970), pp. 143-44. The rejection of polytheism is a continually recurring theme in the Koran.

9. F. M. Denny, "Adhān," in *Abingdon Dictionary of Living Religions,* ed. Keith Crim (Nashville: Abingdon, 1981), p. 3.

number of times. The worshiper utters a prayer for the Prophet and the people in the midst of whom the worshiper performs the *salat*. On Friday, the day of gathering, adult males are required to participate in the noon prayer in the mosque; women may participate in the back of the mosque. Then the sermon is given. The people, who have bowed in surrender to the Exalted One, are confirmed in their responsibility on and for the earth. In this way the prayer combines humility and thankfulness.

In addition to the ritual prayers, there are personal prayers at other important moments of the day, such as the prayer of praise at meal times. There are also spontaneous prayers, thanking God and asking for his forgiveness and support. Thus worship surrounds life from the rising of the sun until it sets. The whole of life is in the possession of *islam*. This internalizing of worship through the regular repetition of bowing before God and prayer strongly resembles the divine offices of the monks — praying from early morning to late at night, singing and being silent before the face of God. The traditional Protestant model of life comes to mind here: a prayer on rising with thanks for the new day and the request for assistance with the tasks of the day, prayers before and after meals, at the beginning of lessons and meetings, and the bedtime prayer, in which the events of the day are brought before God. Through the regularity of such a devout life Muslims are helped to experience their faith truly. They are consciously Muslims in the world.

The effect of the *salat* and the prayers is increased by fasting during the month of Ramadan. It is common knowledge that Islam follows the cycles of the moon, which are somewhat shorter than the Western calendar months, so that the month of Ramadan does not always fall in the same season. Unless sick, one must refrain from food and drink so long as one can distinguish a white and a black thread woven into a fabric. For four weeks one lives very consciously of being a Muslim, thereby internalizing the faith. In addition, a Muslim must (if financially able) make at least one pilgrimage to Mecca in order to participate in the rituals.

Thus social life is enveloped within the religious life, something that is revealed in the duty mentioned last — the giving of alms. True devotion is not simply directing one's face in prayer to the east or the west, but it is believing in God, the day of judgment, the angels, Scripture, and the prophets, and giving money to relatives, orphans, the poor, travelers, and beggars.[10] This rule is detailed later in order to clarify the manner in which it must be applied. It begins with all people being responsible for each other as brothers and sisters. That there is injustice among Muslims does not diminish this rule any more than killing among Christians detracts from the central place of the Sermon on the Mount in the gospel.

That Islam permeates all of life is also evident from the fact that contemplation of the legislation and elaboration of the Koran for life within Islam is certainly as important as theology. Knowledge of both the law and theology are pillars of Islam.[11] The Koran's instructions for concrete living and the oral tradition from the earliest times are specified in a system of laws and regulations. This elaboration gave Islam the label of a legalistic religion in some periods and areas, an image strengthened by the striving for certainty. Skepticism, writes F. Rosenthal, became the worst fear of Muslim civilization.[12] There must be certainty and complete surrender.

The combination of strict obedience and the *sharia* (Islamic law) with certainty could produce steadfast people. Islam spread quickly through consistent witnessing and the desire to fight polytheism and to subject people to God's will. A hundred years after Muhammad's death, Arab Muslims had penetrated deeply into France by way of North Africa and Spain, and large parts of the Balkans were under Islamic rule. In 1529 Muslims were outside the walls of Vienna; until 1913 parts of Yugoslavia were in Turkish hands. It is understandable that Islam is associated with militant actions, yet one should not forget either the scars left by the Christian crusades in the Islamic world or Western colonization. In addition, one must realize that the Muslim community had always offered shelter to Christian and Jewish minorities; throughout the centuries Jews and Christians have been able to practice their religion, constrained only by some limitations where their way of life conflicted with the Koran. Christians who had converted to Islam

10. Sura 2:177.

11. Rosenthal, *Knowledge Triumphant*, p. 239.

12. Ibid., p. 300. Nor was Neo-Calvinism greatly pleased with skepticism; H. Bavinck called doubt the sickness of the soul of our century (*The Certainty of Faith* [St. Catharines, Ontario: Paideia, 1980], p. 8); on A. Kuyper and Bavinck, cf. my "Vast en zeker: Over zekerheid en onzekerheid in het geloof," in *In rapport met de tijd: 100 jaar theologie aan de Vrije Universiteit* (Kampen: Kok, 1980), pp. 257-67.

could not become Christian again; turning away from Islam was and still is forbidden. Yet the Jewish and Christian communities were often secure within these limitations.[13] In Islamic Spain the Jews had less to fear from the Muslims than from the Christian church later on.[14] For this reason the question of who had the most to fear from whom is not easy to answer. In both prophetic traditions — Christianity and Islam — power has been used wrongly to a large extent.

A central issue in interreligious dialogue is whether militancy is justified by the true gospel and by true *islam.* No one can deny that the gospel of the Sermon on the Mount opposes the use of force; crusades, whether in ancient or modern form, do not concur with the essence of Christian belief. The question is whether this is also the case with Islam. At this juncture we must consider *jihad,* which can be translated as "holy war," but means literally "exerting oneself" (i.e., on the pathway to God).[15] This exertion is directed toward the conversion of heathens to the faith: "Fighting is also prescribed for you even though it may seem detestable to you."[16] However, the background and explanation of the text should not be forgotten. With regard to the explanation and its application, one must consider the distinction made between the greater and the lesser jihad. The latter is waged with weapons, whereas the former is the individual's struggle against his or her own evil tendencies.[17] As far as the background of these texts is concerned, one must take into account that the prophet Muhammad was involved in battle due to circumstances. After his call to be a prophet, the circle of his followers remained relatively small. Mecca was a religious trade center and, because he condemned polytheism, Muhammad constituted a threat to the Meccans.[18] After some time, when the opposition became too great, Muhammad fled to Medina (622), where he became the religious leader of a growing

13. See A. Khoury, *Toleranz im Islam* (Munich: Kaiser, 1982); for a few examples of legalization, see my *Religions and the Truth: Philosophical Reflections and Perspectives,* tr. J. W. Rebel (Grand Rapids: Eerdmans; Amsterdam: Rodopi, 1989), pp. 292-93.

14. See R. M. Seltzer, *Jewish People, Jewish Thought* (New York and London: Macmillan, 1980), pp. 342-48, 364-72.

15. See Wessels, *Inleiding,* p. 73.

16. Sura 2:216.

17. A. Wessels, "Muslims, Jews and Christians in the Middle East," *SID* 1 (1991): 87.

18. Wessels, *Inleiding,* p. 35.

community. The conflict between Muhammad's group and his Meccan opponents finally resulted in battle, by which action Muhammad came to be held responsible for armed activity. In 630 Muhammad's men conquered Mecca without too much resistance. During a pilgrimage to the Ka'ba (the holy rock) in Mecca in 631, Muhammad's later successor Ali read aloud a proclamation in which followers were called to war against unbelievers.[19] This struggle centered on the question of people being allowed to worship idols; they were not to give any companions (partners) to God.

This is how Muhammad became involved in armed struggle, and the comparison with Jesus is obvious. Although Jesus never fought, he did cause serious conflicts and, for example, took physical action to purify the temple. In the Old Testament the people of Israel were required to wage war against the Canaanites to purify the land of those who worshiped idols (gods) and those who committed injustices, and the Israelites were permitted to possess their land. Jesus' opponents were not idol worshipers but Jewish priests whose religion is portrayed in the New Testament as too formal and too external. Jesus preached complete trust in God and love of one's neighbor regardless of who that neighbor was. Muhammad had other opponents in a different context, which explains why he took different action.[20] This does not alter the fact that Jesus did not seek earthly power; he stated emphatically that his kingdom was not of this world. The call in the Koran to convert pagans by any possible means is also, in principle, alien to the New Testament.[21]

19. Sura 9:3-28; Wessels, *Inleiding,* p. 39.

20. Cf. K. Cragg in his pioneering book in the area of dialogue, *The Call of the Minaret* (New York and Oxford: Oxford University Press, 1956), p. 302; "force is valid in the Prophet's hand and name," whereas Christ did not take the way of power and opposition. Here lies a fundamental difference between the Koran and the gospel, although one must take into consideration that the Christian church had to contend with the questions of political responsibility, power, and force when the emperor converted in 313. Muhammad accepted those responsibilities.

21. Sura 2:190-91, 216. In Christianity the command from the parable of the great banquet is sometimes — and not by a few — interpreted wrongly and seen as a reason for force: "Go out to the roads and country lanes and make them come in, so that my house will be full" (Luke 14:23, NIV). The Latin translation reads "cogite intrare" ("force them to come in"). Cf. John 18:36. In the passion narrative the "other kingship" of Jesus plays a large role, also specifically in the inscription on the cross: "The King of the Jews" (John 19:19-21).

The Islamic tradition explains the summons to jihad in various ways. Such a given in the holy book of a religious movement always offers multiple possibilities of interpretation. The jihad sometimes led to holy conquest, in which those believers who perished could expect heaven's reward. In addition, as we have seen, a less militant interpretation was possible: service to the way of God and war against one's own imperfection. Just as there are enormous differences within Christianity, so there are differences in the Muslim communities. Sufis emphasize the internalization and experience of God's love and nearness. Fundamentalist Muslims are more militant and stress obedience. In a number of countries whose populations have an Islamic majority, the *sharia* has become the basis for all legislation.[22] In other countries, they strive for this ideal.

With this introductory description, I now consider a number of the points of discussion between Muslims and Christians: faith in God, the prophethood of Muhammad, and the value of the Koran.

4.2 One God, Creator and Ruler of All Things

The most important question for Christian reflection on Islam and dialogue between Muslims and Christians is whether Muslims believe in the same God as Christians. Christians who are not convinced of this shared belief formulate this question as follows: Do Muslims know God? When phrased this way, the question allows two answers. If Muslims do not know God, then Allah is an idol — and does not the Bible itself say, in the Psalms, that God made the world, while the gods of the peoples are idols?[23] If Muslims do know God, then this

---

22. Cf. Christine and Charles Amjad-Ali, "The Shariah Act and the Democratic Process," *SID* 3 (1993): 28-41; for the official pluralistic governmental policy in Indonesia, the Pantacila, see E. M. Sitompul and M. W. Widdwissoeli, "Islam in Indonesia," in *Islam in Asia: Perspectives for Christian-Muslim Encounter*, ed. J. P. Rajashekar and H. S. Wilson (Geneva: Lutheran World Federation and the World Alliance of Reformed Churches, 1992), pp. 85-86, 91-93. One must consider that in many Western countries churches or even state churches actually have a large influence on legislation.

23. "For great is the Lord and most worthy of praise; he is to be feared above all gods. For all the gods of the nations are idols, but the Lord made the heavens" (Ps. 96:4-5).

would seem to be the end of the matter, for what is there left to talk about? The dilemma is posed in this way — either they know God or they do not — but it is a strange dilemma. One could also ask, for example, whether Muslims know God just as well as Jews and Christians; perhaps they know God in a different way, or better, less, or just as well.

Now an immediate objection will be that one can discuss this second question only if the first question is answered positively: only if one assumes that Muslims actually address God (and not a fabrication) can one raise the question of the relationship between their knowledge of God and that of Christians. This is nonsense, however, for the first question cannot be answered without the second. It seems that one must first establish whether Muslims know God in order to ask whether they know God better or less, but the way in which the first question can be answered flows into the second: without knowing what Muslims say about God, one cannot determine whether they know God. Who has the right to determine whether Muslims know God without first verifying just what it is that Muslims believe? The confession of the psalmist is a value judgment based on his many experiences; that which the psalmist has seen in his vicinity with regard to images of gods are idols. For the supposition that Muslims do not know God, Christians sometimes point to texts that connect the knowledge of God or the acquisition of salvation exclusively with Christ.[24]

It would be helpful, for purposes of clarification, to compare this question with the question of whether Jews know God. Christians believe that knowledge of Christ is central for knowledge of God. For most Christians this does not imply that believing Jews who do not believe in Christ do not know God. However, many Christians will seriously question whether Jews know God as well as it is *possible* to know him through Christ. In such a way one can — and must — wonder whether Muslims do not know God and salvation. One cannot answer that question a priori; one must examine what Muslims say about God. That is the first thing I will investigate. In this way one can form a judgment on both the question of whether they know the Creator of heaven and earth as well as the question of whether

---

24. In particular, Acts 4:12: "Salvation is found in no one else, for there is no other name under heaven given to men by which we must be saved."

they know God in a different way, better, or less, or just as well as Christians. Before making that judgment, however, I would like to consider a variant of the reasoning that I have just discussed.

An articulation of the exclusive standpoint in terms of philosophy of religion appears to be as follows: there is only one Being, who has made all (other) things and who is the Most High of all that exists in reality. Christians maintain that this title of Creator and Most High belongs to the Father of Jesus Christ (X), and Muslims maintain that it belongs to him who spoke to Muhammad (Y). The word "God" is, in other words, a unique *title term,* which can belong to only one "someone." Thus the title cannot belong to both X and Y, because, just as a city has only one mayor, so the universe has only one "being" that merits the title "God." That is why, if Muslims are right (and Allah is "God"), then Christians are mistaken, and vice versa. As in Anselm, "God" is therefore defined as "that which nothing greater can be conceived."[25] The importance of this description of God is that it is obvious that one cannot speak noncommittally about God. Because God is the Most High, one must be guided by God in one's life.[26]

This approach appears to lend itself to an exclusive standpoint: either the Muslim or the Christian knows the "being" to whom the title "God" truly belongs. However, this impression is mistaken. "God" is a special title because there is only one to whom this title belongs. One can get a clearer idea of this point by comparing that title with "the president of the United States." While many have been president and others can be (if they are elected), there is only one God, who has not been elected and has no successors — it is actually a title that is entirely unique. That is why the person and the functionary cannot be distinguished from each other in this case. It follows that someone who utters an "incorrect" name yet thinks of "God" when she or he does so (for example, "the one who sustains all things") can still be addressing God even though she or he does not know the correct name.

25. Anselm, "Proslogion," in *The Prayers and Meditations of St. Anselm with the Proslogion,* tr. B. Ward (London: Penguin, 1973), p. 245 (Latin: "aliquid quo maius nihil cogitari potest"). For Anselm's contact with Muslims, see A. Vanderjagt, "Inleiding op Anselmus," in *Over waarheid* (Kampen: Kok Agora, 1990), p. 40.

26. Cf. V. Brümmer, *Theology and Philosophical Inquiry* (London: Macmillan, 1981), pp. 284-85. Also his *Speaking of a Personal God: Essays in Philosophical Theology* (Cambridge: Cambridge University Press, 1992), p. 92.

This is analogous to the situation in which one knows for certain that the person in city hall with whom one speaks is the mayor, even though one does not know his or her name. Just as someone can direct a request to the mayor even though one does not know or is mistaken about the mayor's name, so someone can turn to God without knowing his correct name. In that situation one addresses God, even though one does not know God by the correct or best name (and knows less about God than is possible). One can understand this situation clearly by taking into account not only Muslims and Christians but also Jews. Jews believe that Adonai is "God," Christians call the Father of Jesus Christ "God," and Muslims call Allah "God." Muslims believe that Adonai, the Father, and Allah are one and the same. Many Jews believe that as well.[27] Christians believe that Adonai and the Father are the same, and it is a matter of dispute among Christians as to whether Adonai and Allah refer to the same entity. Thus the question of whether Allah is correctly called "God" leads to the question of whether we think *sufficient reasons* are available to conclude that by Allah Muslims intend Adonai and no one else. Therefore the question of whether Muslims believe in the same God as Christians — that is, if they really believe in God — can be answered only by examining what they believe. Do Christians and Muslims have so much in common with respect to their belief in God that one may reasonably assume that they intend one and the same God? One must thus first examine what is said about God in Islam and, particularly, in the Koran. Here one must continually take account of different emphases and various developments that have taken place within the Muslim community, just as within the Christian churches. I will compare a few characteristics of the Muslim concept of God with what Christians say about God, treating, first, those elements of the concept of God that correspond, and second, the elements that differ.

For Christians one of God's most important attributes is that God offers support and rest. "He who dwells in the shelter of the Most High will rest in the shadow of the Almighty."[28] People can find shelter from the storms of life in the Almighty and the Most High. The great exalted God supports people and is near in trouble. "The eternal God is your

27. See L. Jacobs, *A Jewish Theology* (New York: Behrman, 1973), pp. 284-91.
28. Ps. 91:1.

refuge, and underneath are the everlasting arms."[29] With these words Moses blesses one of the tribes of Israel; if a person succumbs to life's storms, then he or she falls into the hands of God. In grace God takes pity on people. It is precisely God's mercifulness and nearness that are also accentuated in the Koran. The suras are introduced with the words: "In the Name of God, the Merciful, the Compassionate." God forgives mercifully: and if God were to take humans to task for their wrongdoing, he would not leave even one creature that crawls on the earth.[30] God is the Merciful, *'al-Rachim*. He will mercifully guide believers on the right path. The first sura of the Koran is characteristic for the Islamic and Muslim concept of God, which functions like the Lord's Prayer for Christians. The *sura al-fatiha,* the opening sura of the Koran, reads as follows:

> In the Name of God, the Mercy-giving, the Merciful!
>
> Praise be to God, Lord of the Universe,
> the Mercy-giving, the Merciful!
> Ruler on the Day for Repayment!
> You do we worship and you do we call on for help.
> Guide us along the Straight Road,
> the road of those whom You have favored,
> with whom You are not angry,
> nor who are lost!

The belief in God's mercifulness and support and the prayer to be led along the straight path unites Muslims and Christians. For those who seek his face, God is a place of refuge.[31]

Other points of agreement among Christians and Muslims are the awareness that the creation points to God and that God far

---

29. Deut. 33:27a.

30. Sura 16:61.

31. L. Gardet, "Allah," in *The Encyclopedia of Islam,* ed. H. A. R. Gibb et al., new ed. (Leiden: Brill, 1960), under that heading, 1:409; "Refuge": *ma'ab,* for example, in sura 3:14; 78:39; J. H. Kramers, *De Koran* (Amsterdam: Elsevier, 1969[3]), translates 78:39 as "destination" ("bestemming"); Leemhuis, *De Koran* (Houten: Wereldvenster, 1989), as "on the path back to his Lord" ("op de terugweg naar zijn Heer"); and R. Paret, *Der Koran: Übersetzung* (Stuttgart: Kohlhammer, 1989[5]) as "one time with his Lord" ("Einkehr bei seinem Herrn").

transcends human comprehension. According to Muslim theology, God's existence and a few of God's characteristics can be discovered through creation. Here one should remember Paul's words: God's eternal power and divine nature have been clearly seen, being understood from what has been made.[32] This recognition is in line with the Psalms: the heavens declare God's glory, the skies proclaim the work of his hands.[33] The Koran often speaks of the signs of creation that point to the Creator, as in the following passage:

> . . . while those who disbelieve and reject both Our signs and meeting in the Hereafter will be presented with torment.
>
> Glory be to God when you reach evening and when you arise in the morning! Praise Belong to Him throughout Heaven and Earth, and after supper and when you are at your noonhour.
>
> He brings forth the living from the dead, and brings forth the dead from the living, and He revives the earth following its death. Thus shall you (all) be brought forth [again].
>
> Among His signs is [the fact] that He has created you from dust, then you were propagated as human beings.
>
> Among His signs is [the fact] that He has created spouses for you from among yourselves so that you may console yourselves with them. He has planted affection and mercy between you; in that are signs for people who think things over.
>
> Among His signs are the creation of Heaven and Earth, as well as the diversity in your tongues and colors. In that are signs for those who know.
>
> Among His signs are your sleeping at night and by day, and your pursuit of His bounty. In that are signs for any folk who listen.
>
> Among His signs is how He shows you lightning for both fear and anticipation. He sends water down from the sky so He may revive the earth with it following its death. In that are signs for folk who use their reason.
>
> Among His signs are [the fact] that the sky and earth hold firm at His command. Then whenever He calls you forth out of the earth once and for all, you will (all) come forth! Anyone who is in Heaven and Earth belongs to Him; all are subservient to Him.

32. Rom. 1:20.
33. Ps. 19:1.

He is the One Who starts out with creation; then He performs it all over again. It is quite simple for Him [to do]. He sets the Supreme Example in Heaven and Earth; He is the Powerful, the Wise![34]

The world is assessed positively; it contains many signs that point to the powerful, wise, and kind Creator. If people do not see these signs, the fault lies in them themselves. The signs are clear for those who reflect, hear, understand, and believe. Unbelievers do not see these signs, but because the signs are clear they cannot be excused. This same notion plays a large role in the discussion on the text already mentioned by Paul in the letter to the Romans: something of God is evident in creation, but people do not see it.[35] To those who say that Allah could have spoken somewhat more clearly and given a decisive sign, the reply is given: "We have explained signs for folk who are certain."[36] In principle the signs that point to God are visible to everyone. The Koran seems to go farther than Paul with regard to what one can know about God through creation. Paul speaks in that connection of God's eternal power and divine nature, but according to the sura quoted above, the creation shows God's power, wisdom, decisiveness, and benevolence (apparently in regulations that are pleasant for people, such as spouses and sleep).

For Christians a question arises here: Is it not necessary to acknowledge that there is also much in nature that is hostile and incomplete? Nature is ambiguous; life germinates in the seed, but there are also calamities and cruelties. It is questionable whether one can, on the basis of the observation of nature, say more than that the existence of nature is a great riddle that evokes the notion of an origin and a purpose, and that much seems to express some design. How clearly does the ambiguity of nature point to the benevolence of God? Is nature not indifferent with regard to human happiness?[37] Muslims and (most) Christians acknowledge that creation points to God, but there seems to

---

34. Sura 30:16-27; cf. 16:79.
35. For example, H. Kraemer, *Religion and the Christian Faith* (Philadelphia: Westminster, 1957), pp. 300-317.
36. Sura 2:118.
37. T. de Boer, *De God van de Filosofen en de God van Pascal* (Zoetermeer: Meinema, 1989), pp. 88-95.

some difference as to how far God's goodness or benevolence is apparent in nature. In addition to the good in nature there is also much that is destructive for life, under which the whole of creation groans.[38]

God's existence can be clearly seen from nature. The visible world points to God, who is the source of all things, who sustains them, has bestowed on them laws and the delicate ecological system — all of this points to God's power and will behind creation. God "is the First and the Last, the Outward and the Innermost," says the Koran.[39] God is different from humans and remains a mystery. The Bible also emphasizes the difference between God and humans: "For I am God, and not man — the Holy One among you."[40] God exceeds human understanding and in this sense is a mystery; he lives in unapproachable light.[41] A few of God's attributes can be seen in the signs of his majesty, but his being cannot be fathomed. For Muslims God's being remains an inexpressible mystery.[42] Yet God is known in his attributes, and some of God's attributes can be known through the creation. For a deeper and more complete knowledge of God, however, one needs revelation.[43]

Another aspect of the traditional concept of God that Muslims and Christians share is the belief in God as Judge. God sits on the throne, sees all that occurs, and knows what is in people's hearts. God is prepared to forgive, but at the same time he is the Judge who distinguishes between what is right and what is wrong. This concept of God as sitting on the throne speaks more to some Christians than to others. For more secularized Christians it has become somewhat vague; God is more a power that sustains all things than a Judge. Other Christians see God as

---

38. Rom. 8:22.

39. Sura 57:3; Gardet, *Encyclopedia,* 1:408.

40. Hos. 11:9. God's holiness rises from the purity of his action on the one hand, and on the other, from his exaltedness above the existence of his creatures.

41. 1 Tim. 6:16.

42. *ghayb,* Gardet, *Encyclopedia,* 1:409. The different schools of theology and philosophy naturally had different emphases; cf. M. Fakhry, *A History of Islamic Philosophy* (London: Longman, 1983): the Mu'tazilites stressed God's oneness (in the sense of *simplicitas*) and justice and, because of the oneness of God's being, identified with his attributes (p. 45); in contrast, in order to be able to speak about God's attributes, the Asharites proposed that these characteristics are eternal and connected to his being, although they are neither identical to nor different from it (p. 205).

43. Rosenthal, *Knowledge Triumphant,* pp. 130-31, 133, 136-37.

an ally in the struggle against injustice and oppression: he is a comrade in this struggle. Traditionally, the representation of God as Judge has been central for the concept of God in the Western church. It belongs to the piety of the book of Psalms: "The Lord is on his heavenly throne. He observes the sons of men; his eyes examine them."[44] God sees that which is hidden; he knows the depths of the heart[45] and will bring to light what is hidden in the darkness (of the human heart) and expose its motives.[46] In this way God is depicted as the Judge on the throne who sees all and knows all.

This belief is also central in the Koran: ". . . the Mercy-giving [Who is] settled on the Throne";[47] "He is the One Who created Heaven and Earth in six days; then He mounted on the Throne. He knows what penetrates the earth and what issues from it, and what comes down from the sky and what soars up into it. He is with you (all) wherever you may be! God is Observant of anything you do."[48] According to the traditional Muslim teaching about God, God sits on the throne. Some of God's attributes are spoken of anthropomorphically.[49] Thus Muslims and Christians also share the belief that God sees and disapproves of evil deeds and that nothing can be hidden from God. The Koran continually directs people to their responsibility, which is also impressed on them through the many references to judgment after death or at the end of time.[50]

A further correspondence between Muslim and Christian understandings of God is the traditional belief in God's omnipotence as well as in human responsibility. In the history of both Christian and Muslim theology there have been attempts to specify more closely the relation between what God does to people and what persons themselves do. This issue is concerned with the question of whether faith is a gift from God or the work of the individual. On the one hand, there is God, who rules all things, is almighty, and thus able to enforce

44. Ps. 11:4.
45. Ps. 139.
46. 1 Cor. 4:5.
47. Sura 20:5.
48. Sura 57:4.
49. See J. M. S. Baljon, "Qur'anic Anthropomorphisms," *Islamic Studies* 27 (1988): 119-27.
50. I will forego a further discussion of belief in the judgment and its consequences.

his will; God, who reveals himself, gives faith, and thus can cause someone to believe. On the other hand, there is the individual, who is him- or herself responsible, and can do wrong things as well as not believe. If one emphasizes God's omnipotence, then one arrives at a doctrine of (double) predestination: God foreordains some people to be believers and others to be unbelievers. But then the difficulty arises that faith is conditional for eternal salvation while unbelief is cause for eternal punishment. The difficulty here is how people who do not decide for themselves to believe or not can be rewarded or punished. For this reason others do not stress divine predestination but rather the human responsibility in life and faith. People either believe or do not believe, doing so in freedom and on their own responsibility. In this way the reasonableness of reward for belief and punishment for unbelief is justified.

This theological quandary — a fact in monotheism — has occupied Christian as well as Muslim theologians for centuries. Reflection on the relation between God's work and human freedom has yielded views with several nuances. Similar differences of opinions have appeared in Muslim and Christian sides, particularly in the areas where theology has come under the influence of scholastic schools. If the one school stresses that God rules and is in control of all things, then the other stresses human freedom.[51] In this way an attempt is made to safeguard two mutually supplementary truths from the Koran: God's power and human responsibility.[52] God rules wisely and justly; whatever happens to someone is his or her own fault, in spite of divine testing or warning.[53]

It is characteristic of the Muslim concept of God that God's perfection is given ninety-nine different names. These attributes of God are carefully gathered from what the Koran reveals about God and supplemented from the tradition. They are the ninety-nine most beautiful names of God. As an aside, in order to keep people properly humble, humans know ninety-nine names of God — the hundredth name is known only to the camel. Some of these are: the One and

51. For discussion in Christian theology, see G. C. Berkouwer, *Divine Election*, tr. H. Bekker (Grand Rapids: Eerdmans, 1955), for example, pp. 28-29, 32-33.

52. Montgomery Watt, *Bells Inleiding tot de Koran*, p. 145.

53. J. F. McCann, "The Theme of Suffering in the Quran," *Bulletin of the Secretariatus pro Non-Christianos* 73 (1990): 49-51.

the Unique, the Living One, the True and Real One, the Exalted One, the Great One, Light, the Wise One, the Omnipotent, the One who is unequalled by all of creation, the Hearing One, the Seeing One, the Knowing One, the Bountiful, the Certain One, the Protector, the Benevolent One, the Merciful One, the Forgiver, the Merciful, the Well-Disposed One, and the Best Judge.[54] From this it is clear how many of God's attributes are common to both Muslims and Christians: the belief that God is other than human beings, the Creator exalted above creation and distinguished from it, that God knows and sees, that God knows all human actions and the secrets of human hearts and judges these as good or evil. And above all, they share the belief that God is merciful.

Christians and Muslims share many insights. In surrendering in faith and obedience, many Muslims serve as examples to Christians. Even though one may not agree with their further exposition of God's attributes, there is still so much agreement that one may assume that Muslims do refer to God, the merciful Creator and Ruler. Even if there were less agreement among Muslims and Christians, I believe that one could still come to this conclusion, but I discuss this matter in §5.3. This is not to say that Muslims and Christians have the same concept of God. As it happens, one issue causes difficulties for Muslims in relation to Christian discourses about God, and this concerns the central point in Christian belief: the relation between God and Jesus.

4.3 The Relation between God and Jesus

Muslims regard Jesus as a great prophet. God sent numerous messengers to the various peoples, and to the peoples of the Book he sent prophets. Isa, or Jesus, was one of the greatest prophets. In the Koran he is called the Word of God, God's servant, and the Messiah.[55] Thus

54. Montgomery Watt, *Bells Inleiding tot de Koran,* pp. 145-46; Gardet, *Encyclopedia,* 1:408; cf. J. Hick, "Trinity and Incarnation in the Light of Religious Pluralism," in *Three Faiths — One God,* ed. J. Hick and E. S. Meltzer (Albany: State University of New York Press, 1989), p. 201.

55. G. Parrinder, *Jesus in the Qur'ān* (London: Faber and Faber, 1965), pp. 16, 45-48; for a few Islamic texts on Jesus and Jesus' sermons, see M. Ayoub, "Towards an Islamic Christology: An Image of Jesus in Early Shi'i Muslim Literature," *Muslim*

Muslims are able to regard Christians as believers, and are also able to recognize the prophecies of Jesus as the words of God. Yet because of the unity and exaltedness of God, the confession that God is revealed through the actions, dying, and rising of Jesus Christ remains a stumbling block. This is expressed in the passage in which Jesus is called the Word of God:

> People of the Book, do not exaggerate in [practicing] your religion and tell nothing except the Truth about God. Christ Jesus, the son of Mary, was merely God's messenger and His Word which He cast into Mary, and a spirit [proceeding] from Him.
> Believe in God [Alone] and His messengers, and do not say: "Three!" Stopping [it] will be better for you. God is only One God; glory be to Him, beyond His having any son! He owns whatever is in Heaven and whatever is on Earth; God suffices as a Trustee.[56]

This passage from the Koran is directed toward the close relationship of Jesus and God in the Christian tradition and touches on the Trinity (note the mention of "a spirit"). The motives cited for not speaking of the Trinity are the exaltedness and oneness of God, as well as God's being unable to have a child by a woman.[57] The central motive is evidently not a Muslim desire to degrade Jesus to an ordinary human being. It is not common to call Jesus the Word and Spirit of God! Rather, the reason is the exaltedness of God, which is also expressed in the Bible: "God is in heaven and you are on earth, so let your words be few."[58] Here as well one should not say too much: too many words yield foolish talk. If one says too much about God, one oversteps the boundaries of truth. One must limit oneself to the truth — that God is God, he is just and merciful, and he guides the world.

Now one must admit, I think, that the doctrine of the Trinity

---

World 66 (1976): 163-88. Cf. H. Küng, "Islam and the Other Religions: Jesus in the Qur'an: A Christian Response," in Küng et al., *Christianity and the World Religions,* tr. P. Heinegg (Garden City, N.Y.: Doubleday, 1986), pp. 122-27.

56. Sura 4:171; cf. 5:77.

57. See Parrinder, *Jesus in the Qur'ān,* pp. 126, 133-41. In connection with the Trinity, the Koran elsewhere mentions Allah, Jesus, and Mary: sura 5:116. See also A. Wessels, *De moslimse naaste* (Kampen: Kok, 1978), pp. 105-6.

58. Eccl. 5:2.

and the two-natures doctrine can easily be understood as an arrogant way of speaking about God. Sometimes it seems as if Christians know what God's being consists of — one divine substance with three divine persons, the Father, the Son, and the Spirit — and how Jesus is constituted — having two natures, one divine, the other human. Thus, while the Trinity is called a mystery, its structure has been charted.[59] In understanding the Christian doctrine of the Trinity as a sort of "theory about God," the call to respect the boundaries, speak soberly, and limit oneself to the truth goes unheeded. Some forms of the doctrine of God certainly appear to have lost the awareness of submission to God. The doctrine of the Trinity also is not to be viewed as an attempt at a theory about God but rather as a formulation of a confession as to how God has revealed himself. The sura cited states that one must say nothing but the truth about God. This is precisely the issue involved for Christians because the deepest truth about God has become clear in Jesus. In order to become acquainted with the deepest truth about God, one must speak about Jesus. What God is like is revealed in Jesus' cross and resurrection. It is precisely Jesus' cross that, in traditional Koranic exegesis, is incompatible with his status as a prophet: "God lifted him up."[60] This is often interpreted as saying that God does not permit the one he sent to be crucified.[61] It is a question of justice: God does not abandon his prophet. Anton Wessels indicates that a fairly established narrative style of the fates of prophets, and of Muhammad as well, does indeed exist: the prophet encounters opposition, is threatened, yet is ultimately saved by God. Wessels points out, however, that Jesus' death is presupposed in another sura.[62] Taken at face value, therefore, the Koran permits an interpretation other than the usual one and in which it is assumed

59. See T. F. Torrance, *Theological Science* (London: Oxford University Press, 1971²), pp. 207-8; idem, "The Integration of Form in Natural and Theological Science," *Science, Medicine and Man* 1 (1974): 143-72, 165-66.

60. Sura 4:158.

61. See H. Busse, *Die theologischen Beziehungen des Islams zu Judentum und Christentum* (Darmstadt: Wissenschaftliche Buchgesellschaft, 1988), p. 137. On this, see also A. Wessels, "The Experience of the Prophet Mohammed," in *On Sharing Religious Experience,* ed. J. D. Gort et al. (Amsterdam: Rodopi; Grand Rapids: Eerdmans, 1992), pp. 238-42.

62. Wessels, "Experience of the Prophet Mohammed," p. 240; sura 3:55; 19:33 [34]. In addition, sura 4:157-58 is directed against Jewish, not Christian, ideas.

that someone else died in Jesus' place. Nevertheless, the classic Muslim concept of God with its emphasis on God's power is still at odds with the suffering and dying of Jesus Christ. "The suffering Christ remains incomprehensible for Muslims."[63]

Whereas Jesus' crucifixion conflicts with the Muslim way of speaking about God, it is determinative for Christian thought about God — at least as it is viewed broadly in Christian theology. In order to describe this in more detail, I must first clarify the actual meaning of the expression "the cross of Jesus." The expression is an abbreviation: the cross is the central Christian symbol, signifying many things at the same time. The expression "the cross" is itself a symbol, referring to much more than just the wooden cross on which Jesus died: it refers to the long history of God with human beings.

For Islam God is the God of all people; people are his agents and servants, his caliphs, on earth, and he sent many prophets to them. The Bible says that God has a special bond with one people, Israel, with whom he has a long history. As related in the Bible, the cross stands at the end of that history. In the covenant with God the people of Israel took on themselves a special duty that other people did not have. An old story says that the other peoples refused the covenant with God because they could not or would not fulfill basic requirements.[64] What did this covenant consist of? Israel promised to be a righteous people and to serve God. The motive God had for entering a covenant with Israel lay in the injustice that ruled (and still rules) on earth. The purpose of the covenant was that Israel would be a righteous people, so that righteousness and peace would flourish somewhere in the world and so that Israel would have a positive effect on the other peoples. Thus there is, on the one hand, the limitation to one people, the descendants of Abraham (election), and on the other hand, the universal import ("All peoples on earth will be blessed through you").[65] The purpose of the covenant is the *universal* salvation of people; the means of the covenant is the *special* history of God with Israel. The Jewish tradition speaks of the yoke

---

63. Wessels, *De moslimse naaste,* p. 106; cf. p. 127.

64. E. E. Urbach, *The Sages,* tr. I. Abrahams (Jerusalem: Magnes, 1979), 1:532-34.

65. Gen. 12:3; for various interpretations of the calling of the Jewish people that differ greatly from one another, see Jacobs, *Jewish Theology,* pp. 269-75.

of the kingdom: a privilege, a task, and a burden. The history of Israel given in the Tanakh (the Jewish name for what Christians call the Old Testament) makes clear how this goal has not been actualized, hence the significant role of the prophets in Israel: they tried to call people back to the covenant — the way of life of justice and mercy in this concrete world.

Thus an important distinction between the Koran and the Bible is that the Koran does not speak of a covenant between God and a people but rather of the lives of all people before the face of God. The result of this is that the history of God and his people does not stand central in the Koran; it does not concern a salvific history but obedience in faith among all people. The life of the prophet Muhammad is indeed a historic episode, but certainly not an age-long struggle of God with a people. The Koran tells of the prophets and the opposition that they met, just as Jesus met opposition in the Jews and Muhammad in the people of Mecca.[66] But the Koran is set within that which is universally human. It is a message for all people: all people should become Muslims, for God is the sovereign God of all people. This is not the situation given in the Bible. God is indeed the sovereign Lord of the whole world and thus the God of all people, but the path that God had to follow in order to achieve his goal involves a long history of God with Abraham and his descendants. Here Abraham is not first of all a prophet and exemplary believer, but the one to whom God gives his promise that a people shall arise from him who will serve God.[67]

This is a *special* history, the covenantal history of God and Israel, which became a way of suffering. It is a long history in which God calls people — people who hesitantly obey only to turn away after some time and go their own way. The point is not even that people turn away from God but that people also turn away from each other: the just do not prevail and the poor are not helped. From beginning to end, the Old Testament is a book about ordinary life. In the Psalms people complain about the misery to which they have been subjected. The writer of Ecclesiastes has almost given up hope that things will

66. See Wessels, "Experience of the Prophet Mohammed," pp. 233-36.
67. The Koran mentions several times that Abraham received a child although his wife was old (sura 11:71-72); he had two sons (14:39). Abraham was neither Jew nor Christian (3:67-68) and a great and exemplary believer.

be set right, yet he still searches for a satisfactory way to live. Some prophets do not want to prophesy because they believe the situation to be hopeless. They give up — it is almost a lost cause: these people have no ears, "their heart has become fat"; they do not want to hear the truth. Hence the background of this special history lies in the depth and gravity of sin. There is something very wrong with people and they suffer because of one another. At the same time, however, God suffers: God had intended the world to be good and had created it as such, and the creation story continually stresses that what God made is good. God gave people commandments — in Jewish terminology, the Noahic covenant for all people. But it does not seem to work; it descends into chaos. God intervenes and calls Abraham. From the descendant of Abraham and Sarah the people of Israel descend; yet, in spite of the wonderful occurrences throughout, there are constant failures in the Old Testament.[68]

In this world the righteous, who do not live only for themselves, do not have an easy time of it. The recognition that there is friction between the order of this world and the norm of justice is expressed in the later period of Old Testament history. The most moving passages of the Old Testament are the songs of the suffering servant of the Lord. The fourth song begins as follows:

> See, my servant will act wisely; he will be raised and lifted up and highly exalted. Just as there were many who were appalled at him — his appearance was so disfigured beyond that of any man and his form marred beyond human likeness — so will he sprinkle many nations, and kings will shut their mouths because of him. For what they were not told, they will see, and what they have not heard, they will understand.[69]

The question that the prophet poses — after this long history of hope and failure — is what kind of person the true servant of God, the true caliph, will be like. Given this world in which injustice and blindness

68. Once again, I do not deal with the Judaism-Christianity relationship because this is, I believe, different from the relationship of either of these religions to Islam. But what I say about the meaning of Christ does have implications for the relationship between Judaism and Christian faith. One should remember as well that the Jewish community had to carry a heavy yoke through the ages.

69. Isa. 52:13-15.

105

rule, the answer is apparently that the true servant, who is just, inevitably has to suffer much. Someone who lives in harmony with God's will may be an easy victim, but such a life is, contrary to all appearances, a turn for the better. This is insight into "the history of the cross," and is also what happened to Jesus. And for this reason the places where the Koran's interpretation denies the crucifixion of Jesus concern not only the death of Jesus but the entire "history of the cross."

As we have seen, the real point is not simply that the traditional explanation of the Koran happens to state that Jesus did not in fact die on the cross. This would be a discrepancy with the Bible that perhaps does not go too deep, and the explanation of the Koran may even change with time. The difference is more profound, however, for it involves the analysis of what is wrong with this world (the doctrine of sin) and consequently also the analysis of what must occur in order to right the wrongs in the world (the doctrine of salvation). Thus the discrepancy about "the cross" is consequential for the view of human beings, life, sin, and salvation. The "history of the cross" began already with Adam and Eve, where God searches for Adam but cannot find him because he is hiding from God: "Adam, where are you?" This discrepancy also involves insight into who God is.

The New Testament connects the cross of Jesus with God. A classic indication of the relation between Jesus, God, and the path of suffering over many centuries can be found in the parable of the tenants.

> There was a landowner who planted a vineyard. He put a wall around it, dug a winepress in it and built a watchtower. Then he rented the vineyard to some farmers and went away on a journey. When the harvest time approached, he sent his servants to the tenants to collect his fruit.
>
> The tenants seized his servants; they beat one, killed another, and stoned a third. Then he sent other servants to them, more than the first time, and the tenants treated them the same way. Last of all, he sent his son to them. "They will respect my son," he said.
>
> But when the tenants saw the son, they said to each other, "This is the heir. Come, let's kill him and take his inheritance." So they took him and threw him out of the vineyard and killed him.[70]

70. Matt. 21:33-39.

This parable about Jesus' role makes two things clear: (a) Jesus' destiny is related to sin: the tenants are not good caliphs; (b) Jesus is linked with God. I will expound on these points.

The difference between Islam and Christianity regarding "God and the cross" is more than a simple question of facts. It involves an insight in which what is at stake is oneself. If one dissociates "Jesus" from the long story of "the cross" and Muhammad from his struggle with the faith in the one God, then for Christians "Jesus" becomes merely a hook (on which to hang everything), while the same is true for Muhammad as far as Muslims are concerned. Then one need not worry about the difference: both prophets lead different groups to God. But because reference to Jesus involves the long path of the suffering of "the cross," there is much more at stake than simply that Christians refer to Jesus and Muslims to Muhammad. The recognition of Jesus as Lord implies that the Christian believer places him- or herself at the feet of the Crucified One, confessing that "the cross" is the believer's fault. The story of "the cross" concerns both God and people at the same time. People are held responsible; they are tenants, caliphs, of God, but they feel they are the owner of the vineyard and are disobedient to God. On this point Islam and Christian belief differ: the tenants do not allow anything or anyone to change their minds. Here the story runs parallel to what I just said about the true servant of the Lord: people make themselves master of everything and everyone, whereas the true servant of the Lord is someone who no longer fits into this "vineyard," our world. In a last attempt at human self-preservation the tenants kill the son of the lord of the vineyard and say: "The vineyard is ours!"

The consequence of this is that the question of whether Jesus is the true servant of God cannot be answered without first determining whether one is oneself a tenant who does not wish him to live. This is not neutral terrain: "he who is not with me is against me," Jesus said.[71] In the dialogue on the concept of God one must apparently determine for oneself who one is and who one wants to be: whether one is on the side of the tenants/caliphs who want to master this world and transform justice into injustice, or on the side of the true Servant,

---

71. Matt. 12:30. In another context Jesus apparently says something different, namely, with reference to people who do good: for whoever is not against us is for us (Mark 9:40; Luke 9:50).

even though one then no longer completely fits in this world. In short, the question of whether Jesus is the Son of God cannot be answered without forming a judgment as to why people do wrong in this world.

The view of Christ is therefore directly connected to the view of sin and salvation: Jesus' appearance is bound up with sin. In the end the owner of the vineyard sends his own son. The entire past history is linked to this act. The New Testament is not detached from the Old Testament: the coming of Jesus is not a small fragment of divine history, spanning a few years, but an inseparable part of the long "history of the cross." God's Spirit has roused people to protest against injustice throughout the centuries. Again and again people have made themselves master of creation in order to do with it what they will. Even religion was and is not safe from the human striving for power. In other words, within their enterprise the tenants had set up their own religion as well, a religion that had nothing to do with the Lord of the vineyard. One cannot understand the death of Jesus without understanding the gravity of sin. Those who sinned were the caliphs, the tenants, who had accepted their orders from God with rules that were known to them. But they threw out all the commands of prophets, thereby indicating that they would not let anyone or anything tell them not to plunder the vineyard and make their own goals subordinate. The mundane reality of the plundering of the environment and the unjust poverty in the world confirms this message of the Bible.

The parable of the tenants — and numerous other places in the New Testament — associate Jesus with God. The ancient history of God's wrestling with people, in which God attempts to move them to peace, love, and justice, leads to Jesus Christ. Because the initiative of this history of the cross lies with God, people have also sought for the initiative behind Jesus' life and appearance in God. The hand of God has been recognized in the appearance of Jesus: through Jesus God has come among people. This remains a mysterious clue, for the Bible does not speak about God himself having been born as a man, but about his "son" (or "child"). The divine initiative behind Jesus' appearance is told in two Gospels with the story of the virgin birth: Mary becomes pregnant without the assistance of a man, but with the power of the Almighty, who overshadowed her.[72] There is an element

72. See Luke 1 (1:35 in particular) and Matthew 1.

in the story of Jesus' birth that can easily be overlooked if put directly into words. The truth of the story of the virgin birth is that all human initiative is excluded: this child comes — ultimately — from God. It is someone of a different order, so to speak.

The Gospel of John expresses this quite differently — not in the form of a more or less mythological story, but using theological concepts. The Word, by which God has called all created things into existence, has become flesh in Jesus. However one wishes to express it, God came among the people in Jesus. In one sense, Jesus was one with the Father.[73] This can only be comprehended against the background of the glaring injustice and disaster of humankind, the obstinacy of people, and the perversion of religion: God himself provided the true Servant of the Lord. Ultimately, he saw no other possibility than to send his own Child, the only begotten Son. God remains God while he makes himself nothing and simultaneously becomes human. In this way God reveals himself as loving and forgiving. Through the Spirit that remained with people after the death and resurrection of Jesus, God further inspires people to do good.

Belief in Jesus Christ as the Son of God therefore involves the Christian concept of God directly. The Koran states repeatedly that God is powerful, omniscient, full of compassion, and merciful *(rachman)*. The Bible goes one step further: God, the Creator of all things, becomes the Partner of people in their battle for a good life and, in Jesus, ultimately becomes the victim of human obstinacy. Christians themselves find it difficult to comprehend this fully. It often remains a matter of a belief that has not been fully thought out. The problem lies in including both the weakness of God and his majesty, both his love for people and his exalted immortality, both his sovereignty and his dependence on human beings in one concept of God. God is love by showing himself powerless; God comes to the aid of people by suffering their obstinacy; to a great extent the Creator passes the initiative to obstinate people. Thus part of Christian theology has learned to speak gropingly about God, resulting in what is known as *dialectical* theology, that is, theology that states one thing about God, and then states something else that does not completely agree with the earlier statement but supplements and corrects it. I will give two examples.

73. John 14:6; 17:21.

109

God is Almighty, yet things occur that are not willed by God. God's love is endless, yet God holds the sinner responsible. This two-sidedness or dialectical way of speaking about God is most clearly seen when speaking about the Crucified One: Jesus who was crucified on the cross and on the third day rose again from the dead; Jesus is at the same time the Crucified One and the Risen One, the conquered and the conqueror. This is expressed by the use of capitals in the title "the Crucified One." Jesus, the Crucified One, is the image of God, wholly human and, as such, crucified, dead, and buried, but also wholly God and, as such, the Living One. It is impossible to formulate the story of "the cross" and "the resurrection" within a consistent theological theory. God is beyond human comprehension. It is extremely important to realize that the human intellect cannot grasp transcendence.[74] According to the gospel, however, that is not the point: of course the Most High is beyond human comprehension — that does not constitute any reason for amazement. But that which really has not been thought of and transcends knowledge in a completely different way is the love God has for people who always fail.[75] In other words, the heart of God becomes visible in the cross and the resurrection of Jesus.

For this reason speaking about Jesus in his intimate relationship with God and God in his internal relatedness with Jesus is a non-negotiable part of the Christian faith. It is precisely this relationship between God the Father, Jesus, and the Spirit, who proceeds from both, that leads to the doctrine of the Trinity. Both Jews and Muslims question whether the doctrine of the Trinity does not conflict with the oneness of God. This doctrine, however, is misunderstood if viewed as an arrogant way of speaking about that which people cannot know: God's inner being. Speaking about the triune God can (and must, in my opinion) be regarded as a modest, restrained formulation that attempts to remain true to the way in which God has revealed himself, and does not entail any speculation about "God's obscure being" apart from the way in which people have come to know God.

---

74. Cf. Plato's dialogue *Parmenides* and the many writings of the Christian tradition that were influenced heavily by Neoplatonism, particularly those written from the perspective of the *theologia negativa*.

75. Eph. 3:19. Cf. also J. Slomp, ed., *Christenen en moslims in gesprek: een handreiking* (Baarn: Ten Have, 1983), pp. 50-51.

This does not involve philosophical speculation about God's attributes, but rather a confessional speaking about the Creator and Covenant Partner in his relation to the person Jesus Christ and the Spirit through which he works among people.

The idea of the Trinity arises from a number of Bible passages that speak of the oneness of Jesus and the Father as well as of the Comforter who came after Jesus was taken into heaven, and in particular from the so-called baptism formula, which refers to the Father, Son, and Spirit. Jesus tells his disciples to preach the gospel all over the world and to baptize people in the name of the Father, the Son, and the Holy Spirit.[76] The oneness of God and Jesus is expressed quite evocatively in yet another place in the Bible and, because this image is closely related to what I discussed in the preceding section, I repeat it here: the image of God on the throne. We have seen that this depiction of God on the throne is also widespread in Islam. The Revelation of John presents God as sitting on the throne, while those who, like the true Servant of God, have been oppressed on earth stand before the throne and praise God's greatness:

> and he who sits on the throne will spread his tent over them. Never again will they hunger; never again will they thirst. The sun will not beat upon them, nor any scorching heat. For the Lamb at the center of the throne will be their shepherd; he will lead them to springs of living water. And God will wipe away every tear from their eyes.[77]

God is on the throne, and in the middle of the throne is the Lamb, Christ. The "middle" (the heart) of God is, symbolically depicted, God's love. The power of God is his forgiveness in Christ. The cross — the entire human history of trouble and injustice — will pass, for God will wipe the tears from their eyes. The heart of Christian belief lies in this image of the Lamb on the throne, which was rendered so beautifully in the Middle Ages by the van Eyck brothers (in Ghent). Here, against the grain of human nature, the ethics of the Sermon on the Mount (love those who hate you, bless those who curse you) turns out to be the victor over the rule of an eye for an eye, a tooth for a

76. Matt. 28:19; cf. 1 John 5:7.
77. Rev. 7:15-17.

tooth. Here the karmic law (reaping what one has sown in this life, retribution in the next life) is transcended by forgiveness. God forgives people their wrongdoings. The Koran also speaks of God's forgiveness, but the biblical path of forgiveness is longer and proceeds via "the cross." Forgiveness does not come through God's goodness alone but through the history of the cross.

This is why the Bible is a historical book, which was narrated over the course of several centuries and emerged from a history of more than a thousand years. The Bible is about earthly history, not about an overcoming of this world in the divine brahman. Justice and injustice, peace and conflict, hate and love are central; these opposites are not transcended in an experience of unity as they are in *shunyata* or the deeper unity of all things. Muslims and Christians share these views, but, from the perspective of the Christian concept of injustice and human impotence, one must ask of Muslim theology if it is true that people achieve salvation, peace, and justice on their own power. Is it not clear from the newspapers that injustice prevails and that peace is continually violated? The Koran gives a central place to justice and solidarity; lining one's pocket at the expense of others *(riba)* is forbidden. The equality of people and justice were dear to the Prophet's heart.[78] Apparently, however, even laws such as the Ten Commandments and the *sharia* are insufficient to put people on the right track. Sin is not just a transgression of the law — it goes deeper.

The "history of the cross" illustrates the depth of *sin:* something within the hearts of people must change, as Buddhists and mystics also claim. We saw in chapter two that a no-self must replace the wrong "self"; the question was which "self" this is and how the right "self" originates. How does this change come about? If we cannot do it ourselves, it must come from somewhere else. Because there is much suffering, much must be forgiven and redressed. How does this occur and who can accomplish this? At this point one may recall what I wrote at the end of chapter two about what Reformational theology called justification by faith. Justification by faith has to do with the message that, through Christ, God accepts people as they are and that they no longer need to prove themselves or make amends in any way

78. Cf. H. Mintjes, *Social Justice in Islam* (Leusden: Diaconal Bureau of the Reformed Churches in the Netherlands, 1977), pp. 21-29.

whatsoever. We must forego here a fuller exposition of Christian doctrines of reconciliation, justification by faith, human freedom and responsibility. In the dialogue between Christians and Muslims, a Christian must speak of the heart of the gospel: God's love, which on the one hand allows justice to triumph, and on the other is extended to the just and the unjust.

This Christian concept of God, with its roots in the history of God and people, makes it impossible for Christians to develop a simple concept of God. God is one, Christians say with Muslims and Jews. But the one God is also three: He was present as the Creator, he showed himself to be a Covenant Partner and the "Father" (or "Mother") of Jesus Christ, and he works through his Spirit among people. God is Father, Son, and Spirit — three, yet one. What is one in God is three for us: God is simultaneously, nonnegotiably, and essentially Father, Christ, and Spirit. God is not only the Creator and Head of all people *(universal)* but also the Covenant Partner in the *special* history of God with his people. The Christian concept of God is incomplete; God remains, as Muslims also emphasize, a mystery. The greatest mystery, however, is God's love and faithfulness. Whereas Muslims speak of the ninety-nine names of God, Christian doctrine speaks of the Trinity.[79]

I return now to the question of whether Muslims know God just as well as Jews and Christians do. Because Muslims, on the basis of the Koran, worship the Creator, the only God who exists and who is master of all things, and because they also know that God is full of compassion, one can concede that they know God. I would like to add that Christians, on the basis of the gospel, are better *able* to know God than Muslims are. But one must recognize that the depth and intensity of personal faith does not at all depend on the knowledge that the Bible or the Koran gives to someone. It is possible for someone with a lesser knowledge of God's history with people to have a more intense faith. Why should a Muslim who does not know of God's far-reaching love for people in Christ be unable to experience God intensely as loving? Many Muslims bear this out.

---

79. Cf. Hick, "Trinity and Incarnation," p. 201: "the two schemes cover essentially the same ground."

4.4 The Prophet Muhammad

A subsequent question in the Christian reflection on Islam is whether the Koran is God's Word and whether Muhammad is a true prophet. Wilfred C. Smith has discussed the question about the Koran as the Word of God more than once. Smith argues that the Koran is the Word of God for Muslims. He does not intend here simply a descriptive statement in the sense of "Muslims hold the Koran (whether or not correctly) to be the Word of God," but a theological value judgment: the Koran is indeed the Word of God for Muslims; God speaks to Muslims through the Koran. Smith had already anticipated the following question: If God speaks to Muslims through the Koran, can God then also speak to Christians through the Koran? When faced with this question, Smith referred to an incident in his life. At sundown on a ship in the middle of the ocean, having gone through a difficult period, the phrase "He is enough" occurred to him.[80] At that moment it was a Word of God to Smith. He adds that he might also have thought of God's word to Paul: "My grace is sufficient for you."[81] The fact is, however, that it was a word of the Koran that occurred as the Word of God. It is apparently possible for a word from the Koran to be a Word of God for a Christian. What is one to make of that?

When one states that the Koran or a word of the Koran is the Word of God for people, one can mean quite different things. This issue is related to the question of whether Muhammad was a prophet, since according to Islam God gave his Word, the Koran, to the people through the prophet. This section will deal with the question of Muhammad's being a prophet, and the following section with that of the Koran as the Word of God. There are a number of views on the Prophet and the Koran, each with their different nuances. I will mention six, and do so in the form of propositions. The first proposition is negative, while propositions two through five are increasingly positive with respect to Muhammad's being a prophet.

1. Muhammad was a false prophet who incorrectly thought that he met God and received revelations.

---

80. Wilfred Cantwell Smith, "Can Believers Share the Qur'an and the Bible as Word of God?" in *Sharing Religious Experience,* pp. 57-58.
   81. 2 Cor. 12:9.

2. Muhammad was a believer from the nations of the world whose experiences of God are recorded in the Koran.
3. Muhammad was a prophet who witnessed about the one God to people and brought them to *islam* to God; his testimonies about his experiences of God are recorded in the Koran.
4. Muhammad was a prophet who spoke to people in the name of God; his prophecies are recorded in the Koran.
5. The Koran is the definitive revelation of God through the prophet Muhammad to humanity.
6. God can speak through the Koran to Muslims and other people.

Proposition 5 is what Muslims believe. It is not possible for Muslims to endorse propositions 1 and 2, and they would consider propositions 3 and 4 as saying too little if they were not supplemented by proposition 5. Proposition 6 is Smith's view, but it does not entail that the Koran is God's definitive revelation. Propositions 2 and 6 seem plausible to me. I will return to this, but first I want to indicate and comment on a consequence of holding propositions 2 and 6. That one accepts experiences of God (and not pure paganism) to lie behind the Koran makes it possible to associate the words of the Koran with God; but then one must also view the Muslim who prays as someone who prays to God. For example, this obtains for the following prayer taken from the opening sura of the Koran (already cited in the discussion of God's characteristics, §4.2):

> Praise be to God, Lord of the Universe,
> the Mercy-giving, the Merciful!
> Ruler on the Day for Repayment!
> You do we worship and you do we call on for help.
> Guide us along the Straight Road,
> the road of those whom You have favored,
> with whom You are not angry,
> nor who are lost!

This is the daily prayer of Muslims. Muhammad believed and Muslims today believe that God put this prayer in the mouth of Muhammad. It is possible for a Christian to acknowledge this as prayer and to join in, but if a Christian joins in the prayer, he or she interprets it within the framework of his or her individual understanding of faith. The conception that one has of the last judgment need not agree with that of many Muslims, and there may also be differences of opinion as to the groups of people to whom God is gracious. No prayers and professions of faith exist without such personal and contextual interpretations. Each person has her or his own ideas — within the Christian tradition as well. This does not mean that whoever is moved by words of the Koran has to consider the Koran and the Bible as having equal weight or think the same as many Muslims do about the Koran's words. Yet these comments do not alter the fact that whoever accepts proposition 2 assumes that Muhammad had a relationship with God and that texts from the Koran describe his experiences with God. I will return to these divine experiences, but first I will discuss propositions 3 and 4, which claim that Muhammad was a prophet.

Proposition 3 goes one step further than proposition 2: it calls Muhammad a prophet. Is this justifiable from the Christian point of view? It depends on what one understands the term "prophet" to mean. If "prophet" means someone who devotes him- or herself to God, a "man of God," a "woman of God," or else someone who bears witness to others of the one God, Creator and Ruler, then Muhammad was obviously a prophet. But if one wishes to speak of a prophet only within the framework of biblical history, then Muhammad was not a prophet. Hence it is a question of definition: If a Christian says that Muhammad was a prophet, what is meant by "prophet"? It is a simple verifiable fact that Muhammad believed himself to be a prophet and that Muslims acknowledge him to be a prophet, because for them he is the prophet who points them to God. This requires no further discussion. Muhammad has a crucial position within Islam, including Muslim piety. For this reason the question of whether Muhammad can be revered as a prophet is important for the relation between Muslims and Christians.[82]

The Bible distinguishes between true and false prophets. Proposition 3 entails the question of whether one can consider Muhammad a true prophet, while proposition 1 states that Muhammad was a false prophet. What distinguishes true prophets from false ones? Three Old Testament texts address the matter of recognizing false prophecy.

82. For Muhammad's status, see L. Sanneh, "Muhammed's Significance for Christians," *SID* 1 (1991): 25-29, 36-38.

Deuteronomy 18:22 states that a man is a false prophet if his prophecy is not fulfilled. (This does not mean the converse can be said: if it *is* fulfilled, it does not necessarily mean he is a true prophet.) Deuteronomy 13:1-2 says that a false prophet can be recognized if he urges people to follow gods other than the God who brought Israel out of Egypt. God may test the Israelites by means of such a false prophet to see if they love him with all their heart and soul. In ancient Israel, a false prophet who preaches the renunciation of God in this way must be put to death. Jeremiah's criterion for irrefutable proof of a false prophet is that he leads an immoral life: lying, committing adultery, keeping company with evildoers. False prophets prophesy peace for the unrighteous and prosperity for those who do not maintain justice.[83] Among the Israelites the voice of the prophet is continually the voice of Moses: prophets call the people back to the covenant between God and the people Israel.[84] Deuteronomy 18:18 gives a positive description: a true prophet is someone who says all that God commands him to say, someone in whose mouth God puts his own words.

It is clear then that Muhammad cannot simply be equated with the false prophets such as those just described. He does not flatter people and does not say "peace, peace" where there is no peace. He points people to the one God and clearly repudiates idolatry. In short, Muhammad cannot be dismissed simply as a false prophet, even though Christians have often in the past characterized the figure of Muhammad as an immoral person.[85] Whether Muhammad can be called a prophet depends on how narrowly one defines "prophet." If one understands "prophet" to include all those who call people to faith in the one God, the Creator and Ruler of all things, and also calls them to a just life, then Muhammad is a prophet. But if being a prophet is more closely tied to the Bible, then it is more difficult to call Muhammad a prophet. If one follows the characterization of a prophet in Deuteronomy 18:18 — one who speaks words that God has placed in his mouth — then Muhammad's being a prophet is

83. Jer. 23:14, 17; cf. 6:14.
84. See J. A. Motyer, "Prophecy, Prophets, III: True and False Prophets," in *New Bible Dictionary,* ed. J. D. Douglas et al. (London: InterVarsity Fellowship, 1962), pp. 1041-42.
85. Wessels, *De moslimse naaste,* pp. 79-80.

logically connected to the divine origin of the Koran, because then the prophet is someone who says what God bids him to say. It is clear that Muhammad is perceived in this way. Therefore the question is whether Christians are able to profess that the Koran has a divine origin.

One cannot say that the Bible and the Koran are *equally* inspired or that they reveal God in the same way or equally well. This is a question of intellectual integrity and logic, not one of prejudice. On a number of points the Koran (at least in the classic exposition) contradicts the Bible, such as the issue of the death of Jesus on the cross, which I already discussed above. The Koran rejects the central message of the New Testament, Jesus' crucifixion and resurrection, and this message plays no role in the knowledge of God's justice and mercy. Therefore it is logically impossible to regard both the Koran and the New Testament as equally inspired by God. A historical perspective, which is also a recognized complication in Muslim-Christian dialogue, is involved. Western research has compared the Bible and the Koran and ascertained that the Koran borrowed a number of stories and thoughts from biblical traditions. For Western scholars it is clear that the dependence of the later writing (the Koran) on the earlier (the Bible) must be acknowledged. This is extremely difficult for Muslims to do, since they believe that the content of the Koran was revealed by God to Muhammad. The usual view is that God spoke to Muhammad, who communicated these words to his companions. Soon after his death these revelations were collected in writing and were compiled in the Koran. It is a matter of logic that someone who believes that all that stands in the Koran was literally spoken by God to Muhammad must regard as (partially) untrue traditions that conflict with what the Koran says. It is understandable, therefore, that Muslims have said that the Koran is the final truth and thus the Jewish and Christian Scriptures are wrong on some points, as their content does not agree with what God has revealed through Muhammad.[86] For Western scholars — believers and nonbelievers — this explanation is unacceptable, since no basis for it can be found in the history of the Koran's origin. Western Islamologists point to

86. For the perception of Christians and of the Bible in the Koran, cf. J. Jomier, *The Bible and the Koran,* tr. E. P. Arbez (New York: Desclee, 1964), pp. 23-35; Wessels, *De moslimse naaste,* pp. 20-24.

Muhammad's dependence on Jewish and Christian traditions. Because of the differences between the Koran and the New Testament, one cannot accept both of them as the revelation of God in the same way (even if one would wish to do so). For this reason as well a Christian cannot consider Muhammad a prophet in the sense of the classic Muslim understanding, that is, that God placed his words in his mouth. Muhammad had no deep knowledge of the writings of the Old and New Testaments. He was clearly not a biblical prophet. Since this is something we already knew, it does not tell us much.

But must a prophet know the biblical writings? Is it possible to apply the concept "prophet" more widely so that it includes those outside the biblical traditions as well? Suppose that a "prophet outside the Bible" is understood to mean someone who calls people to belief in the one God, the Creator, and to a life where one is concerned about one's neighbor. Such a prophet outside the Bible has experienced something of God, is touched by this experience, and the encounter with God gives his or her existence direction. This person witnesses to others and is in that sense a prophet. Muhammad was such a person. Because the biblical image of God is partially recognizable in the Koran, one can also say that Muhammad experienced God — not an idol, but the one and only God, the Creator of heaven and earth, the merciful Compassionate One, who extends his desire for salvation to all people. Muhammad knew and understood many things. There are other things he could not have known, such as how far God has gone in his love for people. If one remembers how little of the gospel Christians themselves understand and how poorly people heed the Sermon on the Mount, and if one considers the strong surrender in faith of many Muslims to which they are led by Islam and in particular by the Koran, should one then not acknowledge that Muhammad actually did encounter God? Does God not use the Koran to maintain a relation with Muslims? These are, I believe, realistic questions. Can Muhammad then be called a prophet outside the Bible?

The Bible refers constantly to people outside Israel who believed in God and loved justice. There is a long list of such people,[87] includ-

---

87. For that which follows see Gen. 14:19; Exodus 18; Num. 22:6, 35; 23:19; cf. 24:1-9; 1 Kings 10:9; 17:24 (cf. Elisha in Shunem, 2 Kings 4:1ff.; Luke 4:23-27); 2 Kings 5; Acts 10:2. See also Gen. 4:26: "At that time men began to call on the name of the Lord"; see J. C. de Moor, *Uw God is mijn God* (Kampen: Kok, 1983), p. 56.

ing, first of all, people before the time of Abraham such as Enoch, who walked with God. In Abraham's time there was Melchizedek, king of Salem, whom the Bible calls a priest of God the Almighty, and by whom Abraham allows himself to be blessed. In this blessing Melchizedek mentions God, the creator of heaven and earth. Jethro, the priest of Midian and father-in-law of Moses, tells Moses how to govern the people of Israel. God speaks to the seer Balaam, to whom is given the power that those he blesses are blessed, and those he curses are cursed. On his way to the place where he is to curse the people of Israel, he is stopped by the angel of the Lord; rather than curse he must bless: "speak only what I tell you." Here is a seer outside Israel used by God to speak the truth about peoples who will be blessed and who will perish; his prophecy is directed not toward Israel but toward the unbelieving king of Moab. The non-Jewish seer is used by God to bring a message from the Almighty to non-Jews. The queen of Sheba visits King Solomon, praises his wisdom and his just rule, but above all the Lord God who loves Israel. The widow of Zarephath, whose hospitality Elijah enjoys, comes to belief in God — an episode mentioned by Jesus himself in his preaching in Nazareth in order to criticize the link people made between his hometown and himself and the link people made between God and Israel. The healing of Naaman is another example of God's goodness toward a non-Israelite resulting in the worship of God outside Israel. One might ask how specifically biblical and Jewish the book of Job is. Does Job not involve reflections that could occur to all those who believe in God and righteousness? The prophet Jonah is sent to Nineveh, where the people repent and God does not punish them. If Jonah could have evaded his task (which he attempted to do), could God not have caused another person from outside Israel to prophesy ruin unless they repented? Jonah was a prophet, but would someone else from among the pagans not have been a prophet? When the people of Nineveh repented, mourned, and called to God, did they call to God (or to an idol)? To digress for a moment, has not God inspired people in many places in the course of the centuries to stand up for justice, peace, and compassion?

The New Testament refers to Cornelius, a Roman officer, who is called a godly man, giving alms and praying regularly. The rabbinic tradition speaks of the righteous among the people, people who believe in God and respect the Noahic commandments. People who live righteously and believingly before the face of God have a real rela-

120

tionship with God. (One should note here that Maimonides had a much narrower view of this issue.)[88] The Bible deals with many believers outside Israel and the church. Assuming that Muslims believe in God, then Muhammad also had a relationship with God. He prophesied against the worship of idols and moved people to a righteous and compassionate life. Therefore he was a prophet (outside the Bible). In view of the fact that Muhammad desired to be part of the line of the biblical traditions (for as far as he knew them), one could also say that he was a postbiblical prophet. While on the one hand Muhammad's limited knowledge of the Bible is evidence of a difficulty, on the other hand it is a basis for respect. Although he was not well versed in the biblical writings, he understood that God is One, that people are equal and should be allowed to live in righteousness and peace. In this way he is not a biblical prophet, yet he is a deeply believing person and a postbiblical prophet. His witness is recorded in the Koran. With this point, from the beginning of this section I have by argumentative means supported propositions 2 and 3. The question remains whether Muhammad can be said to have spoken on behalf of God and whether God revealed himself to Muhammad (cf. proposition 4). Christians believe that the Bible was inspired; can Christians say the same now of the Koran?

4.5 Is the Koran Inspired?

One cannot answer this question without going into the meaning of the concepts of revelation and inspiration. The question cannot be answered by a simple yes or no. Various views of inspiration are maintained with regard to the Bible, with a main distinction made between mechanical and organic inspiration. Mechanical inspiration entails a kind of dictation of the Bible by or because of God, sometimes portrayed in paintings by an angel whispering the Gospel in the ear of the evangelist. In this case the biblical authors are clerks who note what God says to them or allows them to say. Islam also includes the doctrine of mechanical inspiration. There is, for example, the classical notion of a heavenly, eternal Koran, which God dictated in bits and

88. See Jacobs, *Jewish Theology,* pp. 289ff.

pieces to Muhammad.[89] A doctrine of revelation such as this leads to a fairly strict and uniform application of the content of the holy book in the community of believers.

The doctrine of mechanical inspiration was popular in Christian post-Reformational theology.[90] People such as Abraham Kuyper and Herman Bavinck have rejected the doctrine of mechanical inspiration. On the basis of the differences between the Gospels, some unclarities in the text of the Bible, historical-critical research, and other facts external to the Bible, scholars deduced that the writers of the books of the Bible themselves played an active role as authors.[91] To give a few examples, Luke's particular way of thinking can be seen in his Gospel; John has a completely different way of thinking and therefore his message is his own: he wishes to clarify other matters than those clarified by Luke, Mark, and Matthew. Hence it was recognized that the authors were "organs," used by God, and this came to be called the doctrine of organic inspiration.[92] This doctrine can be elaborated in different ways; it is possible for the contribution of the biblical authors to be personal to a greater or lesser degree. In the last century, orthodox theology in the Netherlands shifted from a narrow to a broader doctrine of inspiration. Meticulous and reverent biblical research brought to light how much the writers of the biblical books left their own mark on their writings. The books are their testimonies of what they experienced (historical books and Gospels) or their expressions of the experience of belief (for example, the Psalms). The testimony has gone through their thoughts and feelings; they were the *organs* that the Holy Spirit used in revelation. In short, the history of the cross is a long history of many events to which people witnessed in their own way.

Whoever rejects mechanical inspiration with regard to the Bible

89. Montgomery Watt, *Bells Inleiding tot de Koran,* pp. 163-65.

90. See H. Heppe and E. Bizer, *Die Dogmatik der evangelisch-reformirten Kirche: Dargestellt und aus den Quellen belegt* (Neukirchen: Neukirchener Verlag, 1958²), pp. 18-19.

91. Cf. G. Ebeling, "The Significance of the Critical Historical Method for Church and Theology in Protestantism," in Ebeling, *Word and Faith,* tr. J. W. Leitch (Philadelphia: Fortress, 1973), pp. 17-61.

92. For a more thorough discussion of aspects of and developments in the matter of doctrine of Scripture and theological hermeneutics, see my "De gelezen Schrift," in *Honderd jaar theologie: Aspecten van een eeuw theologie in de Gereformeerde Kerken in Nederland,* ed. M. E. Brinkman (Kampen: Kok, 1992), pp. 96-160; and my "Scripture Read and Interpreted," *Calvin Theological Journal* 28 (1993): 352-71.

cannot then accept it for the Koran. Christians and Western scholars in general believe there are some inaccuracies in the Koran,[93] and for this reason alone one cannot assume that the Koran is a divine dictation to Muhammad. The proposition that the Koran has not borrowed anything from Jewish and Christian traditions but is an original Islamic tradition is not acceptable to Western historical-critical research or to Christian theology.[94] Muhammad's dependence on what he knew of Jews and Christians is considered an established fact. A revelation from God to Christians (in the New Testament) and a special revelation with equal claim to Muhammad (the Koran) is impossible because the books contradict each other on some central points. It is impossible for Christians to recognize the Koran's divine origin as it is understood in classic Islamic theology for both philological-historical and logical reasons.

But this is not all that can be said. If the Koran cannot be accepted as a divine dictation (the Bible is not either), can one then say from a Christian point of view that the Koran is a type of organic inspiration? That would entail Muhammad's having intense experiences of God and realizing that God spoke to him, gave him orders, and guided his life. The term "organic" then means that Muhammad, as a person and as a believer, left his mark on his witness. He used sources (such as reports on the biblical history of Jews and Christians) and gave his opinion on a large number of matters, but he borrowed the inspiration for his surrender and obedience in faith from his experience of the Most High himself. Thus the words of the Koran were not whispered to him by an angel, but he himself — on the basis of his experience of God in the stillness of the cave as well as what he had heard about the Bible from others — wrote the prophecies and described how God met him as the Righteous One, the Knowing One, the Judge, and the great Compassionate One.

To the degree in which one as a Christian recognizes oneself in the content of the various sections of the Koran, one may feel addressed by it. Where Muhammad expresses true faith and gives evidence of true insight into life, the Koran will be read with reverence

93. A number of points can be found in D. S. Attema, *De Koran* (Kampen: Kok, 1962), pp. 126-28.
94. Cf. S. H. Nasr, *Sufi Essays* (London: Allen and Unwin, 1972), p. 134 ("common transcendent archetype").

and respect. One may respect it because so many Muslims hear the word of God when they read the Koran. Where one recognizes the God of the Bible, the verses of the Koran may be acknowledged to have their origin in Muhammad's meeting with the living God.

In my opinion the Koranic verses are not words literally spoken by God to Muhammad, but neither are the biblical prophecies. The Spirit's inspiration does not consist of words that are actually spoken, but rather of thoughts and suggestions so enlightening that for people it is as if God simply spoke to them. Thus the Koranic verses can also be viewed as the result of reflections on God's meeting with Muhammad. As such, they can be read with great respect.

With regard to content the Koran differs from the Bible. The latter is the result of a centuries-long history of God's association with people. Both the story of the suffering servant of the Lord and the story of Jesus Christ have a depth that is not encountered elsewhere in the religious world, including the Koran, even though there are penetrating testimonies of people who have evidently understood much. The gospel of the cross sheds a light on people, the world, and God that is not found elsewhere. For this reason the gospel of Jesus Christ is unique and is not interchangeable with other religious traditions. God is revealed in Jesus Christ in a way that cannot be known through the Koran.

Whether one can say that the Koran is inspired is a troublesome question because it is not a cut-and-dried issue. Inspiration is not so much an established quality as a matter of the Spirit of God having moved people to write down their experiences and the insight acquired through those experiences, and having used these writings to reach people. Muhammad experienced God's nearness and had the sense of being given a command. A prophet is not a mouthpiece of God but someone who is overwhelmed by God's nearness, whose entire existence is marked by this experience, and who, on the basis of this, actualizes God's compassion within the situation in which she or he lives.[95] Thus one can say that the Koran does point to the one God, who desires righteousness and is merciful. If inspiration is understood to mean that a holy book plays a role in the relation between God and people, then one could call the Koran inspired.[96] But that

95. A. Heschel, *The Prophets: An Introduction* (1962; reprint New York and London: Harper & Row, 1969), pp. 25-26.
96. I. Vempeny, "Inspiration in the Non-Biblical Scriptures," *Word and Worship*

God can speak to people through the Koran (proposition 6) is not to say that people can learn to know God through the Koran just as well as they can through the gospel.

The profession of biblical inspiration also states that one may trust that what is said there is true. But this is not a strict, uniform given either. Many Christians assume that some biblical stories do not directly express the will of God.[97] The New Testament sometimes distances itself from statements of the Old Testament and offers a reinterpretation of many of the Old Testament prophecies.[98] The New Testament is also time-bound with respect to, for example, the man-woman relationship, and thus is not the Word of God in a simple, literal way. For this reason the concept "Word of God" is generally no longer used. In Reformation theology itself the Scripture was seen as the record of (preceding) revelations. Thus the Bible is a time-bound reflection and consideration of revelation. Since Karl Barth it has become common to view the concept Word of God as having three references: (1) the revealed Word of God, Jesus Christ; (2) the Holy Scripture (as a witness of revelation); and (3) the proclamation of the gospel in preaching (in the broadest sense of the word).[99] The

---

6 (1973): 163-73: because God's desire for universal salvation extends to all people, they are part of God's plan of salvation in Christ. God also works outside Christianity, and non-Christian religions are the result of God's "private" revelation in history; because nonbiblical holy writings are constituent elements in religions outside Christianity, they are "co-authored" by God: "And consequently, they too are truly yet analogically inspired by God in spite of the fact that the message contained in them, as in the case of the OT, is imperfect and waiting for fulfilment" (p. 173, the final words of his article). Vempeny does not explain what "analogous inspiration" means. The reason for his hesitation in calling them ("ordinarily") inspired lies, of course, in their imperfection. If the heart of God has become visible in Jesus Christ, then the Koran cannot be regarded as equal to the Bible. But then it also cannot be said that God is the coauthor of the Koran, the Bhagavad Gita, and the Heart-Sutra.

97. A famous example is the story of Elisha cursing the jeering youths (and their death by two bears) in 2 Kings 2:23-25. There are many more such stories that people have questioned, both in New Testament times and today.

98. Already by relating Old Testament prophecies to Christ. Cf. also Jesus' contradiction of hating one's enemy in the Sermon on the Mount, Matt. 5:43-44; cf. Ps. 137:8-9. Consider here that also the Talmud and later Judaism (re)interpret the Tanakh (Old Testament).

99. See Heppe and Bizer, *Dogmatik,* p. 17; Karl Barth *Church Dogmatics* I/1, tr. G. W. Bromiley, ed. Bromiley and T. F. Torrance (Edinburgh: T. & T. Clark, 1975²), p. 121.

prologue to the Gospel of John has caused the concept Word of God to be closely identified with Christ, which is why it is difficult for Christians to call the Koran the Word of God, even though some acknowledge that God can speak to Muslims and other people through the Koran — just as it is impossible for Muslims to call Jesus the Son of God in the Christian sense of the expression.

It is also difficult to acknowledge with proposition 4 that Muhammad acted on the command of God in everything; Christians do not say that of David or of the prophets in all aspects — they claim it only of Christ. God is revealed in Christ. The Bible is a revelation because the Scripture testifies about Christ. The authority of the Bible is also related to its content, Jesus Christ and his crucifixion.[100] For this reason, even though God's presence and thus the activity of God's Spirit is recognized behind the Koran, it is still difficult to say that the Koran is inspired or that the prophet acted on God's command. This does not concern the denial of the Koran's background in the working of God's Spirit and the divine command given to Muhammad; the objection is that, by speaking in the same terms about the Bible and the Koran, about Christ and Muhammad, one blurs the distinctions. Muslims feel that Christians believe things about Jesus (Isa) that did not occur and things about God that are not true. Christians feel that Muslims do not see a number of matters signifying an essential deepening of faith in God. Accepting a divine command to the prophet or the inspiration of the Koran as divine would minimize the difference between Muslims and Christians. Muslims and Christians cannot make it that easy for themselves; differences should be clarified. Instead of making a crude opposition between Islam and Christianity, Christians would do better to learn to explain what is so special about the history of the cross and resurrection of Jesus Christ.

100. See my "De gelezen Schrift," pp. 146-47, 153-54; also my "Scripture Read and Interpreted," pp. 352-71.

5

... No Other Gods ...

5.1 Introduction

In the previous chapters I discussed central ideas of Buddhism, Hinduism, and Islam and compared them to Christian views. In this last chapter I deal with a number of general questions. I have chosen to discuss questions of belief first and then questions of method, that is, first dialogue with respect to content and then reflections on this dialogue. "The proof of the pudding is in the eating": outside the context of concrete arguments, discussion of the how of argumentation is a rather dry affair. I begin this chapter by discussing a few probable objections to a view such as the one offered in this book. From the one side are the objections against *absolutism* and *exclusivism*, which would be implied by some uniquely Christian convictions(§2). Next, I examine more closely the question that has already been discussed in previous chapters: Are references to God references to the same God? I then make the question more general: Do all religions know the same God (§3)? Next comes the objection from the other side: Christian exclusivity is sacrificed for the sake of dialogue; does not the first of the Ten Commandments say, "You shall have no other gods before me nor shall you worship them" (§4)? This leads to the question of whether Christianity is truly best (§5). Finally, I once again summarize what *critical dialogue* entails; what are its possibilities, what are its criteria, what is its nature and worth (§6)?

5.2 Absolutism or Exclusivism?

The Christian faith allows for a deeper knowledge of God than the Koran, according to the argument made in §4.3. This means that the Christian faith has something that others do not. If God has made his true essence known through Jesus Christ's crucifixion and resurrection, then his true essence cannot be entirely known from the Koran. The Koran speaks of God's compassion but not of Jesus' crucifixion and resurrection. This proposition implies that there is something unique and nonnegotiable about Jesus Christ, and such a truth claim is often viewed as exclusive and absolute. There are many objections to such accentuation of Christian uniqueness, and John Hick words these in a striking way. In a contribution to a conference that included Muslims, Jews, and Christians, he has described the consequences of Christology that are regarded as unacceptable:

> If God has revealed himself in the person of Jesus, all other revelations are thereby marginalised as inferior and secondary. Indeed their effect can only be to draw people in a different direction, away from God's direct self-disclosure in Christ. For if the Creator has personally come down to earth and founded his own religion, embodied in the Christian Church, he must surely want all human beings to become part of that Church. Indeed it would seem to follow that sooner or later they *must* become part of it if they are to participate in the eternal life of the redeemed. Thus the doctrine that Jesus was none other than God himself — or, more precisely, that he was the Second Person of the divine Trinity living a human life — leads by an inevitable logic to Christian absolutism, a logic that was manifested historically in the development of the dogma *Extra ecclesiam nulla salus* (Outside the Church, no salvation).[1]

Hick rightly lodges an objection here against the idea that God has begun his own religious store and that other religions are rival chain stores that have fine window displays but have goods of lesser quality.

---

1. J. Hick, "Trinity and Incarnation in the Light of Religious Pluralism," in *Three Faiths — One God,* ed. Hick and E. S. Meltzer (Albany: State University of New York Press, 1989), p. 204. See also Hick's "Jesus and the World Religions," in *The Myth of God Incarnate,* ed. Hick (London: SCM, 1978[5]), pp. 167-85.

Hick's formulation undoubtedly embodies the objections of many people.

Hick's reasoning conceals a transition from a discussion of the matters of fact to unacceptable consequences of behavior. It first concerns the question of whether something *is* that way, that is, whether God really *has* revealed himself in Jesus, and then possible consequences that are unacceptable. These consequences are initially regarded as *possible* but are later labeled *unavoidable:* Hick speaks of an "inevitable logic." This inevitability would become apparent from the history of the church, and particularly from the development of the dogma "outside the church, no salvation." Hick posits that the belief that the second person of the Trinity has revealed himself as a human inevitably leads to Christian absolutism, and, unfortunately, this has often been the case; whether it is inevitable, however, is doubtful. There is much that demands clarification, and I will introduce a number of distinctions in order to focus the discussion more.

All four of the religions discussed in this book believe that their conceptions conform most to the truth. It is not only Christian absolutism that is at issue here. Does not the notion that the Koran is the definitive Word of God lead with inevitable logic to the idea that sooner or later everyone must accept the Koran? Does not the idea of the dharma in combination with karma and reincarnation inevitably lead to the notion that for a good reincarnation every person must fulfill the duties of the dharma so that good karma is achieved? If enlightenment is attained through meditation and the realization of no-self, then must not every person sooner or later become a Buddhist? In short, exclusiveness is part and parcel of religious truth claims in general and are not solely the property of Christianity. If, like Hick, one wants to eliminate the absolute, exclusive content of belief and discard it, then what is left of religion? I believe that this would result in religious people agreeing on something that is no longer of interest to anyone. Although I am greatly sympathetic to Hick's goal — the advancement of peace, humility, and an orientation toward the transcendent — I do not see what is left of religion if everything that is distinctive is deleted. Moreover, there will always be differences of opinion; the relativist, the humanist, the socialist, and the nihilist have little in common with one another, let alone with believers of any kind. Furthermore, they all have their own individual traits and therefore each has something exclusive.

In Hick's argument one sees a transition from what a belief states to possible or even inevitable (yet unacceptable) consequences of holding this belief. Hick's argument can be summarized in four propositions:

(a) The assertion P [that what the New Testament says about God is true] is an absolute claim to truth.

(b) If person A declares assertion P to be the absolute truth, then in the eyes of person A, person B does not know the truth if person B does not believe P.

(c) The absolute claim to truth inevitably implies that knowledge concerning God, people, and the world is the exclusive possession of the one who endorses that absolute claim to truth.

(d) In order to attain salvation, person B must be a member of the community that has the exclusive truth at its disposal.

From (a) one can see that it is not only Christian claims to absoluteness that are at issue; if one deletes the words between the brackets, it is evident that this proposition refers to all absolute truth claims. I will analyze these propositions in successive order:

(a) the concept of an absolute truth claim;
(b) if A knows the truth, then B does not;
(c) the exclusiveness of religious truth;
(d) the exclusiveness of salvation.

(a) Absolute truth claims?

Truth concerns true knowledge, but knowledge has other aspects as well. In the discussion on religious truth claims, it is not clear which aspects of knowledge are meant. One can distinguish several meanings of "religious truth," but to what does one refer when one talks about absolute truth claims? In what follows I distinguish a number of aspects of knowledge (paying particular attention to religious knowledge) that I have discussed more fully in other works. I begin with knowledge in general, and then continue with religious truth.

Knowledge has a subjective aspect and an objective aspect, neither of which can be separated from the other. All knowledge is

130

personal knowledge, both subjective and objective. The tree in front of my window primarily has meaning for me within my horizon of experience: the buds in the spring, the birds that perch in it, the autumn colors. Things exist as they are experienced.[2] The actual tree is not "real-in-itself," so that my experience of it would be an addition to it; the tree is real in the relations in which it exists and consequently has many aspects, a primary aspect being that it has diverse meanings for people and animals. The tree-in-itself is an oak, but it could have been a maple. So one can indeed distinguish between a subjective and a more objective aspect of the tree. An oak can produce acorns but not chestnuts, independent of our experience and depending only on the type of tree. The objective aspect is primarily important for the biologist, who knows how the tree "works," how nourishment is transferred from the soil into the trunk, branches, and leaves, and how the leaves use light to make oxygen. This is usually called more objective knowledge since it concerns the tree-in-itself. The heavy accent placed on "objective knowledge" raises the misconception from which our technocratic society suffers: the tree is viewed in the first place as a thing, to be analyzed (by the biologist) and to be marketed (by the lumber industry), not first as part of the whole of nature and the whole of reality. If one understands that "objective" means the way the object really is, then *real* objective knowledge of the tree is not knowledge of the aspects of the tree, but knowledge of the tree in the relations in which it exists. Thus the tree-creeper that eats the insects from the trunk and the squirrel that gathers acorns also belong to the "being" of the oak.

Ultimately, then, broad relationships are involved; what are the relationships in which the tree or nature exists? This is a philosophical question. What is at issue here is not the "objective" aspect of entities. Religion is not concerned about studying the "tree-in-itself": one can leave the biological aspect to the biologist and its market value to the economist. But the question of whether all the trees may be cut down is not a question of biology or economics. All things exist in a broader framework — this framework being the area of religion and philosophy, which are concerned with the broad relationships from which all

2. As C. A. van Peursen expressed it in a lecture, they are "communicative"; see his *Verhaal en Werkelijkheid* (Kampen: Kok; Kapellen: Peckelmans, 1992), and earlier studies.

things derive their particular significance. All of these aspects together — the biological, the economic, and so on — as well as the broad relationships in which the thing exists, can be called its *objective side*. Alongside this, one could call how a particular object has meaning for people the *subjective side*. But the objective side and subjective side are sides of the same coin: the subjective and the objective together actually form one whole. Thus if a specific tree has a particular meaning for somebody, then that meaning belongs to the reality in which the tree and the person exist; it is not an arbitrary subjective supplement to a thing that is complete in itself. The tree as pure object is not the real tree, but *less* than the real tree — a tree that has been *object*ified.

Before dealing with religious truth claims, I want to take an intermediary step and discuss the exegesis of written (religious) texts. The written text has its own structure.[3] It has its own objectivity and certainty: a text about Muhammad is not about Buddha. In exegesis and religious studies holy books can be interpreted, although the primary reading and explanation of holy books is in the domain of the communities of believers. These books are read primarily by people who experience something through them. They say something about the broad relationships in which life exists, and whoever wishes to understand this must be personally involved in reading them.[4] But is that not subjective? Contrary to what is often thought, this subjective aspect of personal reading is not arbitrary, but is the condition for discovering their meaning. The meaning is accessible only through personal appropriation.[5] Scholarly exegesis retains some distance from the actual intention of the text. It is an understanding of the text that proceeds by research and inquiry, studying primarily the "objective" aspect of the texts. If an impartial Islamologist reads that Muhammad said we may not give God companions (place idols next to God), then as a student of literature studies, the Islamologist does not ask himself whether he gives God companions; it is even possible that the question of his own personal faith in God does not arise. He is satisfied with

3. Cf. P. Ricoeur, "What Is a Text? Explanation and Understanding," in *Hermeneutics and the Human Sciences*, ed. and tr. J. B. Thompson (Cambridge: Cambridge University Press, 1981), pp. 145-64.

4. See W. Brueggeman, *Texts under Negotiation* (Minneapolis: Fortress, 1993).

5. Cf. my *De Schrift alleen?* (Kampen: Kok, 1979²), pp. 28-31, 222-70; my *Naar Letter en Geest: Over het Beroep op de Bijbel* (Kampen: Kok, 1981), pp. 91-122; and my "Scripture Read and Interpreted," *Calvin Theological Journal* 28 (1993): 352-71.

the discovery that it is clear as to what Muhammad means by giving companions, and clarifies this somewhat with bits of information about the polytheism in Mecca where Muhammad grew up. Those are extraordinarily interesting facts; such commentary is often capable of clarifying texts and bringing them to life. In the meantime, however, it remains a clarification — just a clarification, no more — and is not the message of the text itself. This good literary scholar has not even really read the text, because the text "intends" to ask the reader — him or her — whether he or she actually obeys God. The real text is the text in direct communication; an interpretation within the horizon of the past is only a phase in the process of understanding.

This can be seen in two other examples. Suppose somebody suddenly cries "Fire!" The exegete is like someone who offers an elaborate explanation of what fire is and under which circumstances the speaker of that word now uses it. The real hearers of the message do not take the time for that; they run out of the building, shut the doors, call the fire department, and look to see if there is anything they can do. For the latter, questioning the speaker's meaning rises only if there is no fire at all. The direct meaning differs from the objective meaning.

This does not detract from the fact that exegesis is an enormous help in understanding texts, as one can see in the following example. If the protecting varnish on a painting is no longer clear, it is removed and (sometimes) replaced. Just as restoration replaces the dull varnish, so exegesis can free one from prejudices (which sometimes lie over the text like an unclear layer); furthermore, exegesis can point to many things in the painting through which one can learn to see better and thereby value it more. The subjective and the objective are inseparable. The subjective understanding of the Bible cannot be detached from the objective explanation of the Bible, but it has a different concern. The Bible commentator investigates matters to do with the text and explains them; the believer either agrees with them or wrestles with them. Knowledge of holy books has an objective side and a subjective side.

Now I want to look at religious knowledge itself. In the introduction I stated that a tradition has an identity of its own. Islam is not Islam without the Koran and the Prophet, just as Buddhism is not Buddhism without detachment and Buddha. Hence there are some fixed points, but the explanation of the basic insights of the traditions can be changed because it is contextual. In addition, people vary in their views: not everything is just as important for everyone, which is why people view things differently. This plurality of appropriation allows for belief to be personal as well as for religious traditions to survive changes. Accordingly, belief also has a more descriptive (objective) aspect: *insights* that present the tradition as true and trustworthy. This aspect is the traditional doctrine (which new generations of believers must appropriate), the more or less public doctrine that foreigners can understand to a large degree. I call it the *doctrina*. It is the tradition: insights that are transferred in changing forms and passed down throughout generations with continually changing accents. Related to this is the aspect of lived belief, that is, the belief as it plays a role in a person's life. I call this the (appropriated) *lived religion*.[6] Knowledge of belief has the same structure as all knowledge; it has an objective side as well as a subjective side. Neither can be completely separated from the other. Knowledge of belief is also always knowledge in *personal involvement*.

With regard to claims of the truth of religion, the central question is what is actually meant: Does one think of the *doctrina* or the *lived faith?* One might understand the "truth of religion" to mean that the *doctrina* is true, and in this way one presumes that confessional writings or official ecclesiastical doctrine expressions are infallible truth. The doctrinal formulations of the Roman Catholic Church were traditionally supplemented by the anathema formula, that is, the condemning of those who maintained the opposite. With respect to this, John Hick is right: this is an absolute truth claim that entails the damnation of those who think differently. But this is not a good view of religious knowledge since it does not have an accurate perception of the personal side of the content of faith. This view holds that the truth can be displayed, and the truth claims then have to do with the formulated doctrine. But does this then mean that the entire doctrine is absolutely

6. In *Religions and the Truth: Philosophical Reflections and Perspectives,* tr. J. W. Rebel (Grand Rapids: Eerdmans; Amsterdam: Rodopi, 1989), I have distinguished four meanings of the concept "truth": the public doctrine *(doctrina),* the well-understood doctrine *(veritas),* the lived belief *(religio vera),* and the more or less mystical experience of the truth *(intellectus verus)* — without showing that the last would necessarily belong to everyone's belief (pp. 302-17). For the argumentation here it is enough to distinguish two, although the well-understood doctrine is discussed implicitly later.

true and that everyone must believe the entire doctrine in order to attain salvation? One cannot deny that doctrine is unclear on particular points and that a number of earlier doctrines have been superseded by later insights. Some doctrines are also more central than others, such as the doctrine of *anatman,* "That art thou," the doctrine that there is only one God, and the doctrine of the resurrection of Jesus Christ. Yet these central truths of the four religions discussed in this book are meaningless truths if they are simply displayed. Doctrine is concerned with the objective side of belief, yet it is worthless without the subjective side, which is realized in personal appropriation. The truth of the living belief does not simply lie in formulations. The latter are not unimportant — they concern the objective side of belief — but neither do they constitute the entire truth of belief.

Just as truth claims of one's faith do not simply relate to formulations, conversely, the lived faith alone cannot make any claims to absolute truth. Who would want to say that her or his personal belief is absolute truth? Belief entails convictions about how reality *is*. This truth claim gets lost if truth is understood to be simply what someone wants to believe. Then it would no longer matter what one believes because belief would be private in the strictest sense. Consequently, belief would no longer make sense. Faith knowledge is personal, but it also has an objective side.[7] In this way one can see that truth claims may not be separated from the subjective side of belief, but neither can they be separated from the objective side. If someone says "the truth lies in the highest subjectivity," I would be willing to agree insofar that the descriptive side of belief receives its rightful place in extensive personal involvement.

Therefore it does not appear to be a simple matter to state what the absolute truth claims of religion would concern. It is not easy to indicate the relation between the objective and subjective aspects of the knowledge of belief. There is an age-old question of whether the best dogmatician is the best believer. Is the best exegete necessarily the one who understands the Koran or the gospel the best? Or is the best believer one who trusts greatly in God and reads the texts piously, even though she or he does not have a good exegetical interpretation

---

7. It involves knowledge of reality, even though this knowledge is usually articulated in metaphors and stories. Cf. the so-called realism debate in the discussion on religious knowledge.

of them? Which is the absolute truth — the exegetical truth, the dogmatic truth, or the personal truth? It is impossible to choose among these, and this is why it is not at all clear what a person means by "absolute truth in belief." The understanding of faith has a more intellectual aspect, a more emotional/personal aspect, and a more contextual aspect. But if one does not wish to make an absolute claim regarding *the* truth of "the doctrine" of "the church" (exactly which one?), then one must mean something less defined. In this way one could speak of the truth of the gospel or the truth of the dharma. In other words, the gospel, the dharma, the Koran, or so on contain fundamental insights. A truth claim would then entail that fundamental insights depict things as they really are.[8] This is why such insights, which are said to be *universally valid,* are in principle important for each person.

A religion's claim to truth, however, does not mean that that religious tradition knows all there is to know. The relation between the insights of one tradition and the insights of another tradition must be determined more closely. If they exclude each other, then they cannot all be completely true; I will go into this in more detail later. Thus religious traditions claim that their central insights contain universal truth, which is other than religions claiming to "possess" the entire truth exclusively and absolutely. In chapter four I described how, according to Christian belief, God — his love, goodness, and faithfulness — is profoundly visible in the appearance, death, and resurrection of Jesus Christ. This is a fundamental insight into existence that has many consequences for ordinary life, implying a claim to truth. The knowledge of God through Jesus is, in one respect, exclusive: whatever is unique is always exclusive in a way. The gospel can be called absolute in the sense that the most profound truth about God, people, and the world can be known in Christ. But the word "absolute" is often used in another way, namely, to claim that Christians possess the entire truth — they need not learn anything from others nor are they able to, since the belief of others is always less valuable or even entirely untrue. This view of the absoluteness of Christianity is, in my opinion, incorrect. Christianity is not the absolute religion; Christians *are,* however, able to testify about what, in

8. Cf. my *Religions and the Truth* for an explanation on truth in religion and the place of doctrine; the description of the truth of doctrine is on pp. 356-57.

their conviction, is fundamental (and, in that sense, absolute): Jesus Christ, and his crucifixion. That testimony differs from claiming that what Christians think and what the church teaches is the entire and absolute truth. I expound on that point in the following section. Absolute truth claims have two sides: the belief that is under discussion among people and the logic of the content of belief. I now look at these two points.

(b) If A knows the truth, then B does not

The absolute truth claim can be formulated as follows:

(b) If person A declares P to be the absolute truth, then in person A's opinion, person B does not know the truth if person B does not believe P.

In order to test this claim, I will distinguish between two kinds of situations. First, there are "are you driving, or am I?" situations. The sticker "are you driving, or am I?" means that the passenger must keep his or her opinions to him- or herself; the driver is behind the wheel and must drive smoothly. Second, there are situations in which the driver must pull over and both travelers must get the map out and attempt to determine where they are and which way they must take. A good conversation on philosophy is comparable not to "are you driving, or am I?" but rather to "where are we and where do we go?" In countries where freedom of religion exists, all are allowed to have their own opinions (as long as they do not harm anyone else). Dialogue does not entail forcing a person to accept another opinion, but trying to understand the fundamental convictions of the other person and, if possible, to acquire a little more insight together. Who is right does not matter, but what is true does.

The question of what is ultimately true about God and people does not lead to boasting about one's own religious tradition but to a mutual searching for insight and for a good way of life and living together. Certainly the revelation of Christ — the true *servant* of the Lord — does not involve boasting about the revelation. Mary, Fatima, and Ruth are not situated on a field between the church, the mosque, and the synagogue, where they argue about who has a hold on the truth. Ruth testifies to the covenant with Abraham and the way of her people through the centuries, while Fatima witnesses to the greatness of God and his word in the Koran, and Mary testifies to the love of God that appears in Christ. It is not Jewish, Islamic, or Christian absolutism that is involved, but rather the insight in God, his intentions, and life in general. (Unfortunately, this has often been turned into Christian absolutism; one of the motives for this book is to help prevent that — not only because the consequences of such absolutism are serious but also because such absolutism conflicts with the gospel itself.) The question is not "am I right or are you right?" but whether it is true that God has involved himself with human beings and revealed himself in Jesus in a very deep and unique way, or whether it is true that God forgives the sins of those who repent and desire justice. The question is not whether I and my fellow believer have a hold on the truth and are the best believers, but rather whether the Crucified One is the Resurrected One. It is possible that Mary is a very poor believer but that her testimony is true. Conversely, Fatima can be deeply faithful — an example to Mary in many ways — while the knowledge that she receives from the Koran is less deep than the knowledge available to Mary in the Bible. Whether insight is true does not depend on the person of the believer. Mary does not claim that she has a monopoly on truth, but that the insight to which she has arrived is true. The equality of people before the law does not mean that everyone is all right. Differences of opinion will continue to exist until all people agree or until no one believes anything any more. Every difference of opinion presupposes that a person can differ in opinion *about something*. Knowledge has a descriptive side, an objective side. On these bases I reject:

The Egalitarian Fallacy: because the beliefs of people are equally valid, no one can claim a special status for his or her belief; that is why God has not revealed himself to anyone in a special way.

(c) Does one belief exclude the other?

In connection with the objective side of belief the question arises as to whether one belief excludes the other. One person believes theory P, another theory Q. If P is true, is Q not false? By wording it this way, it is immediately obvious that this conclusion is not valid. Viewed logically, P only excludes the belief "not-P" and Q excludes "not-Q"; whether they exclude each other fully or partly depends on the relation between the content of P and Q. Belief does not involve simply one claim, but an entire cluster of fundamental insights.[9] Christian belief entails, among other things, belief in God as the Creator, human responsibility, the importance of peace and justice in the world, several elements of Jesus' message, the love and goodness of God. These basic insights of Christian belief are related yet do not form a rigid theory. Similar remarks can be made with regard to other traditions. Thus Christians do not believe in one claim but in an aggregate of insights, P. That Muslims also believe in a collection of insights, Q, does not establish that cluster P excludes all belief contents of cluster Q. In chapter four we saw that *overlappings* exist. Muslims and Christians believe that God called Abraham to be a forerunner, that Jesus had a very special relationship with God, that God is compassionate and just, and so on. In short, the cluster of belief contents P overlaps with cluster Q.

But *differences* also exist between the belief content of P and Q, and therefore P and Q do not coincide. Moreover, there are discrepancies between the gospel and the usual Koran explanation concerning Jesus' crucifixion. With reference to vital sections of the belief content, there is an important difference, which is why Christians can say that Muslims (and Muslims can say that Christians) see some things correctly, other things incorrectly, and have no knowledge at all of some matters. Apparently the one belief does not (absolutely) exclude the other. Although this holds for some sections of the belief, it does not hold for the entire belief. The discussion between Muslims and Christians quickly becomes concentrated on the differences, often with the result that little attention is paid to the points of agreement. Because the gospel asserts that the depths of God are revealed in Christ, Christian views do differ from Muslim views. From the Muslim perspective, Christology endangers the confession of God's oneness and exaltedness.

In dialogue with Buddhists and Hindus, Christians encounter

9. I have expanded on these thoughts, with more examples given, in *Religions and the Truth*, pp. 325-29, 339-42, 382-85. For a discussion of the antithesis between belief traditions based on the fact that they would form "entities" or would have derived from (controversial) origins, see *Religions and the Truth*, pp. 321-25, 379ff.; and my "Does Theology Presuppose Faith?" *Scottish Journal of Theology* 45 (1992): 147ff.

other similarities and differences. With respect to spirituality, a number of Christian schools are related to forms of Buddhist spirituality. Since belief entails not one claim but an entire range of beliefs that are more or less related with respect to content, and practices that can be partially shared with others, one belief does not appear to exclude another entirely.

Thus the truth of the message with respect to Jesus does not necessarily lead to Christian absolutism. It does not follow that people other than Christians have no knowledge about God. For this reason the uniqueness of God's revelation implies neither Christian absolutism nor exclusivism, and this is why I reject:

The Exclusivist Fallacy: Because God revealed himself in a special way to some people, these people know the entire truth and other people do not know the truth at all.

In contrast, I posit:

The Thesis of Potential Overlapping: Religious traditions can partially share insights and differ; the existence of differences implies the possibility that one tradition has more insight into the truth than another.

(d) Is salvation exclusive?

The question remains whether, if more than one religion has elements of truth, salvation can be acquired exclusively within one tradition. Part of the answer to this question parallels that of the previous one. Think of salvation in this life; it may be incomplete, fragmentary salvation, yet it is of utmost importance. Who would want to trivialize inner peace, a feeling of stability, and a way of existing in life? Whoever thinks only of absolute salvation (in whatever form) here can easily construe antitheses. If belief P provides salvation only in religion K, then those who would seek salvation must become followers of religion K. But if salvation is analyzed in components and not thought of only as absolute salvation, then it is possible to acknowledge that other religions are also able to provide people with specific forms of salvation in their lives. Buddhist equanimity, compassion, and wisdom as described in the conquering of good and evil can be viewed as a form of salvation, even if the enlightenment raises the danger of the relativization of good and evil. Are the peace that a yogi finds in meditation and the happiness that a Hindu finds in a village festival not real peace and real happiness? Elements of salvation can also "overlap" and be shared. This is an initial answer and I limit myself to this, since any further elaboration would simply parallel that which is explained above.

There are still other considerations. God is the God of all people, and the Bible demonstrates that his concern for human beings involves more people than simply Israel or the church. The boundaries of God's involvement with humans and Israel or the church are not the same. People who believe and those who believe somewhat less belong to the church, as well as people who have understood much or little of the matter. The boundaries of the kingdom of God are not necessarily equivalent to those of the church. Did Christ not say: "I have other sheep that are not of this sheep pen"?[10] In chapter four I listed an entire series of people outside Judaism and the church who are regarded as believers in the Bible. Salvation does apparently exist outside the church. Thus the doctrine "extra ecclesiam nulla salus" ("outside the church, no salvation") is not an essential implication of the belief that God revealed himself most completely in Jesus.[11] The idea that one must view the attainment of salvation not as something earned but rather as a gift from God flows from what has been said in relation to Buddhist and Islamic views on self-analysis and self-justification. The goodness of God that is visible in Christ makes it highly unlikely — and even inconceivable — that God does not work outside the limits of the church as well. J. H. Bavinck states that God's concern reaches out to every person; Buddha would not have meditated on the path to salvation if God had not touched him; Muhammad would not have spoken a prophetic message if God had not been involved with him. "Every religion contains, somehow, the silent work

10. John 10:16.
11. For a short survey of the development of the doctrine of "extra ecclesiam nulla salus" and criticism of it, see H. Küng, *The Church,* tr. R. and R. Ockenden (New York: Image, 1967), pp. 403-11. Küng argues that its positive significance must be stressed: within the church, salvation! Cf. also G. C. Berkouwer, *The Church,* tr. James E. Davison (Grand Rapids: Eerdmans, 1976), 1:138-64. Berkouwer mentions places in *Enchiridion Symbolorum,* ed. H. Denzinger and A. Schönmetzer (Freiburg: Herder, 1965, 33rd printing), nos. 570b, 1000, 1473, 1677.

of God."[12] Bavinck says that people suppress this silent work of God, which causes many distortions of religion — and within Christian communities the distortion of the truth is not unusual. In spite of this, one can acknowledge the beneficial influence of many religious traditions on their cultures.[13] The question of eternal salvation will ultimately have to be left to God. Yet who can doubt that God has poured out his salvation much more broadly than most people would have done?

One could therefore replace the thesis *outside the church, no salvation* with the thesis *outside Christ, no salvation*. After all, if the heart of God is revealed in Christ and if Christ in a sense *is* the heart of God, then God's salvation is always Christ's salvation. And this is the crux of Hick's objection to Christian exclusivism. He posits that the view of Jesus as the second person of the Trinity inevitably leads to Christian exclusivism, since, if people want to be saved, they must eventually become part of the Christian church. Yet it does not follow from the thesis *outside Christ, no salvation* that people must be part of the church in order to be saved. If we are to envision a new earth, it must be an earth without a church, since God will be all in all. According to the Revelation of John, people will praise Christ as the Lamb. Perhaps people who were Buddhist or Muslim while they lived had not ever expected that they would praise Christ, but they will not have to become members of the Christian church to do so. They will learn a few things they do not know at this moment, but I am afraid that that holds for Christians as well.

In the meantime, it is normal for people to hope that other people will learn to share their fundamental insights in existence, precisely because these insights are related to that which is wholesome and

12. J. H. Bavinck, *The Church Between the Temple and the Mosque* (Grand Rapids: Eerdmans, 1966), p. 200. Cf. H. Kraemer, *Religion and the Christian Faith* (Philadelphia: Westminster, 1957), p. 350: "All religions are huge systems of manifold, partly more or less positive, partly more or less negative, responses to God"; cf. pp. 316-17. Cf. K. Runia, *Het evangelie en de vele religies* (Kampen: Kok, 1990), p. 72.

13. J. Verkuyl, *Zijn alle godsdiensten gelijk?* (Kampen: Kok, 1981[4]), p. 110. For the development of the approach to other believers in the Faculty of Theology at the Free University, cf. D. C. Mulder, "Van Elenctiek naar Godsdienstwetenschap," in C. Augustine et al., *In rapport met de tijd: 100 jaar theologie aan de Vrije Universiteit* (Kampen: Kok, 1980), pp. 182-97; and my "Van Antithese naar Ontmoeting," *Gereformeerd Theologisch Tijdschrift* 91 (1991): 122-37.

good. A Christian may hope that others will be convinced of the truth of the gospel or at least learn a little bit of it. Thus it is also normal for a Buddhist to say (as I was once told): "Be a good Christian, and in your next life, I am sure you will be a Buddhist." This is more sympathetic than saying: "*Zazen* leads to enlightenment, but it is not your style; just stick to being a Christian." There is nothing wrong with a Christian hoping that another will discover who Christ is, or with a Muslim hoping that another will take the Prophet's message to heart. As soon as there is pressure to do so, however, it is wrong. Salvation does not involve pressure. What Hick says — if the Creator revealed himself in Christ, all other religions are secondary and inferior — is a real danger. With each religious group there is always the danger of distorting religion and misusing power. How often has the church not been subservient to those in power or become an end in itself? In the quotation given, Hick does not mention the cross of Jesus. Yet, if one considers "the history of the cross," it is difficult to say with Hick, "the Creator has personally come down to earth and founded his own religion." That is not how it happened: Jesus did not found a religion. He was killed on the cross, after which God raised him from the dead. Christianity arose from testimonies to this fact by others, and Jesus cannot be reproached for the misuse of Christianity and the distortion of his message. Nevertheless, one would do well to take note of Hick's warning against Christian triumphalism.

5.3 The Same God?

The previous section concluded that the Christian faith is able to acknowledge that other religions may contain true insights and may be the source of much good, both within the community as a whole and with respect to individuals, and can therefore provide salvation. The use of the word "may" is inevitable. Religion is often misused, and there are many religious schools whose truth and value cannot be seen. Slogans like "all religions are equal," "every religion has equal meaning," and "all religions bring salvation" can be thrown out. There is too much chaff among the grain. Not everything is good, let alone equally good. A person who says that "all philosophies are equally true" agrees with both the believer and the atheist. In short, whoever does not dare to ask a few critical questions here sticks his or her head in the sand. This section draws together a few of the lines discussed earlier; I will concentrate on the issue of whether all religions worship the same God. I dealt with this question already when I compared *shunyata* and faith in God, and I discussed explicitly the question of whether Muslims and Christians believe in the same God. I now discuss the question in general.[14]

How can one find an answer to the question of whether all religions worship the same God? When I discussed the relationship between Allah and the biblical God, I assumed that the two concepts of Gòd would have to correspond sufficiently in order to justify the conclusion that Christians and Muslims worship the same God. But what is sufficient? As far as Islam is concerned the question has already been answered, but it has not been answered for Hindus, and this is what I must discuss now. I first discuss the manner in which I will arrive at an answer, and I then examine the question with regard to content. The greatest difficulty lies in the hermeneutical question of whether concepts from different religious traditions have the same meaning. With respect to this question I also reject the false dilemma that terms in different traditions are either identical or incomparable: they overlap and they can be compared.

Within a concept of God, God is given attributes. A tradition's stories and rituals do this in part implicitly, and sometimes explicitly as well, as in eulogies. The meanings of these attributes are explained within the tradition's rituals, holy books, and stories, which leads to a problem. Sometimes a tradition is viewed as a systematic whole, within which words have their meaning. Consequently, a religion is seen as a "language game" that determines absolutely the meanings of all words. Religious traditions are thus individual rival language games, and thereby incomparable. If this were the case, then one could not become acquainted with religions since becoming acquainted with something unfamiliar always involves a comparison with the familiar.[15] Moreover, religious traditions

14. Cf. my "Do All Religions Worship the Same God?" *Religious Studies* 26 (1990): 73-90.

15. See A. F. Droogers, "Cultural Relativism and Universal Human Rights," in *Human Rights and Religious Values: An Uneasy Relationship?* ed. A. Na'im et al. (Amsterdam: Rodopi; Grand Rapids: Eerdmans, 1995), pp. 78-90. In order to combat

and cultures influence each other; hence the reference to contextual African or Asian theology, and so on. For example, Asian theology is influenced by dialogue with Hindus and Buddhists. Wilfred C. Smith cites a beautiful instance of mutual influence (and overlapping): a Muslim story about a saint, adopted by Christianity, stems from the story of the Buddha. Religions are very different, says Smith, but they are all part of one history.[16] Therefore religious traditions cannot be seen as entirely separate from one another, and are not incomparable.

Another mistake that one can make is to assume that concepts from different traditions are equivalent. Various words from different languages and cultures are translated by the same English term, and one assumes that they mean the same — an assumption that is completely wrong because the meanings of words are determined by their context. It has been demonstrated in biblical exegesis how much a word can differ in meaning when used in the various books of the Bible. What I have said about the content of belief — the possibility of overlapping — can also be said about the meanings of words. Similar words and concepts are comparable; their meanings overlap and there is both agreement and discrepancy. Even though the English translation of the Tanakh (Old Testament) states that God is merciful, and the English translation of the Koran states that God is merciful, one may not conclude that the biblical concept of God's mercy is equivalent to the concept in the Koran. One must be conscious of subtle differences. Note the remarks I made on the comparison of compassion *(karuna)* and love of one's neighbor *(agape)* (§2.4.).

Terms from various traditions cannot simply be considered equivalent; to say that the meaning of words is completely contextual and that the word "compassionate" in the Bible means something essentially different from "compassionate" in the Koran is going too far. Whoever looks more closely — as did the translator of the Koran who assumed he could use the English word "merciful" — reads that people can rely on God's compassion if they have done something wrong or are in trouble; God comes to their aid, and forgives much. Compassion has to do with similar human situations. For this reason

relativism and incomparability, Droogers points to the possibility of becoming acquainted with other cultures.

16. W. C. Smith, *Towards a World Theology* (London: Macmillan, 1981), pp. 6-10; this story is the story of Saint Barlaam and Jehoshaphat.

it is possible to understand what is going on and at the same time to understand that God has an attribute — mercifulness — which is important in that kind of situation. The middle line between the two extremes of incomparability and identification entails the recognition of similarities and differences. "Mercy" in the Koran is not altogether different from "mercy" in the Bible, but neither is it wholly the same. A person wanting to research this thoroughly would have to describe and compare the connections in which "mercy" appears in the Bible and in the Koran, thereby obtaining a differentiated representation of the concept of God in the Koran and in the Bible and attaining a better view of the similarities and differences. The same goes for *agape* and *karuna*. This example may serve to make clear that one must avoid the two extremes of the all-or-nothing reasoning (words from various traditions are either identical or dissimilar). One can compare the concept of God in two religions by the attributes each religion ascribes to God. One determines whether religions refer to the same God on the basis of what they say about God.

Are there sufficient grounds to say that all religions worship the same God? It all depends on what one understands by "God." One of the most well-known descriptions of God is "that which nothing greater can be conceived," which was already discussed in §4.2. This description is unsuitable as an indication of all forms of transcendence. It can, I believe, be applied to the brahman, but not to *shunyata*. After all, *shunyata* is not higher or better, but simply this reality without the conceptions and psychic connections that belong to samsara: samsara is nirvana. There are also problems with regard to Christian belief. The description is Anselm's and the concept of God in this definition is strongly influenced by Platonism; the greatest is the being that exists of and through itself and is therefore necessary. That being is good, the highest good that lacks nothing, and is thus the perfect being.[17] Anselm sometimes gives as a definition "that than which nothing *greater* can be thought" but explains it as that than which nothing *better* can be thought.[18] The divine, therefore, involves that which a person

---

17. L. M. de Rijk, *Middeleeuwse Wijsbegeerte* (Assen: Van Gorcum, 1981^2), p. 158.

18. Anselm, *Proslogion,* ch. 3, whereas God's attributes (which must "flesh out" the indefinite "greater" [*maius*] in terms of "better") are defined: "For if someone's mind could think of something better than you, the creature would rise higher than its creator and would judge its creator; which is clearly absurd"; cf. ch. 5.

cannot conceive, which is greater and better than what a person can conceive. God cannot be thought; in itself this is a valuable element in this description of God: God is not defined but there is reference to God. The name of God refers to what is irreducible, which to a large degree explains the attraction of this description of God.[19]

The central question is what one must understand by "Most High" or "best." Is the Creator the Most High, the highest being, pure being itself? If the Creator *is* and the created *is,* why is not *being* itself the greatest and best — this is what a Hindu would ask. The description "than which nothing can be thought" lies closer to pantheistic than theistic concepts of God; the latter always make a distinction between God and the world. Anselm avoids this conclusion by giving a Christian fleshing out of "greater" and "better."[20] If God is being, then God is the being of the world; being is divine, and therefore eternal and ultimately complete. The rest is contingent, everything that passes away and therefore can not-be, is not (or is less) real and in this sense is maya, simultaneously real in earthly experience *and* "illusion." Within the Christian faith God must be regarded as Covenant Partner and Creator, as I stressed in chapter three on Hindu faith.

If by God one means the Creator of the world, who gives or has given the world a particular solidity through regularity in nature, then one assumes a concept of God with at least a will and hence a goal, and thereby with attributes usually ascribed to people. Here qualities are involved: creative, willing, purposeful, and (thus) personal (in any sense of the word).[21] If religions ascribe these attributes to God, then one can

19. Cf. T. de Boer, *De God van de Filosofen en de God van Pascal* (Zoetermeer: Meinema, 1989), pp. 42-49.

20. Anselm gives a series of further characteristics of God, such as "that which exists alone over all things, and has made everything out of nothing"; "the highest good, through whom all other good exists"; "just, true, blessed, and whatever is better to be than not to be" (ch. 5). But that is precisely the question: How do we know for certain what good characteristics are? Anselm says that it is "better to be capable of perception, omnipotent, merciful, and impassible" (ch. 6). But why is it not better to be complete in oneself, unaware of the trouble that surrounds one?

21. Compare the qualifications that H. Bavinck introduces with "person" in *The Doctrine of God,* tr. and ed. W. Hendriksen (Grand Rapids: Eerdmans, 1951), p. 301: the divine being does not exist other than as "tripersonal because the *divine, absolute* personality requires this."

assume that they mean the same God, although they differ in their beliefs about God.[22] One can subsequently determine concretely what people say about God. Here I will examine a few examples I have given in another article.[23] If a Jew says "Adonai is the Creator of all things," and a Muslim says "Allah is the Creator of all things," they are not talking about mortals such as David and Ali, nor are they arguing over the question of which of the two created the earth. They are speaking about the Eternal One, the Creator, and are discussing the issue of which names must be given to the Creator and which stories must be told about God. Therefore they speak of the same "subject" although their ideas about "God" may differ. If the Buem and Akkan people in Ghana call the transcendent Nyankopon Kokurako (the Almighty God), Oboadee (Creator), and Nyame (the Radiant), and regard it as Ohuntahunu (the All-Seeing God), Nyansabuakwa (the All-Wise), and Ahofamado (the All-Loving), then one can conclude that these people intend the same God as Jews and Christians.[24] If a Zen master states that faith in God is only halfway down the road to ultimate wisdom because the idea of a separate being, distinguished from the world in which we live, is naive and betrays attachment to the self, then I see no philosophical ground for concluding that Zen and Christianity refer to the same divine or "empty" transcendence.

In view of the many different ideas about God, it is remarkable that the attribute of goodness is often ascribed to God. I have intentionally not added goodness as an established attribute, because, after all, it all depends on what is understood by goodness and on which grounds goodness is ascribed to God. If the goodness of God concerns goodness in relation to human beings (and other living creatures), one

---

22. I will not take up further implications of these four characteristics (such as "being conscious") here, as we are concerned with a minimal description (which allows various elaborations). Thus it is possible for various views of "Creator" to overlap partially. A further analysis would require a study in the field of the philosophical doctrine of God. My point here (in order to hold to "Creator") is simply that if two people have different ideas about "Creator," that is not to say that these ideas are entirely dissimilar. These ideas have some common elements, and it is in this sense that they overlap.

23. In my "Do All Religions Worship the Same God?" p. 88.

24. J. K. Ansah, "The Names and Concepts of God Among the Buem and the Akkan of Ghana," in *Naming God,* ed. R. P. Scharlemann (New York: Paragon House, 1985), pp. 90-92.

can say that people mean the same God. If, however, God's goodness means a goodness that is turned into itself, in the sense of an inner perfection indifferent to everything else, then in my opinion another concept of goodness and another concept of God is involved. If attributes such as having a will and purpose and maintaining relations with people, other living creatures, or things in the world are not ascribed to the divinity, then people mean a different divinity. A remote, self-sufficient divinity cannot be identical to the Creator and Covenant Partner who is concerned with things.[25] Such concepts of God do exist, and thus the question of whether all religions know and worship the same God must be answered negatively.

Nonetheless, the various ideas of the highest, the eternal, or the transcendent are comparable, because they always concern that which ultimately grounds reality and at the same time that toward which one must direct oneself in life.[26] One may call this *the transcendent* because it transcends the (ordinary) world. The various images of transcendence are comparable insofar that they refer to (a) what transcends and grounds the visible world, and therefore to (b) that on which human fulfillment depends and in which one can find salvation. For these reasons the ideas of the transcendent are comparable. Transcendence is therefore a theoretical term that one uses in order to be able to compare ideas on the divine, God, gods, and emptiness. Transcendence is therefore not being or a being but a heading, a human category, necessary in the discussion on what reality ultimately sustains. Thus what believers agree on is that the horizontal reality that we are able to see and that we try to manipulate is not the most important, that it is not the ground of itself and us, and that reality is different from the way it often seems. Behind and in reality there is a secret that we call transcendence. Zen Buddhists say that that transcendence is this reality itself, and thus that *shunyata* does not lie behind reality (but is reality itself, merely experienced differently). Advaita

25. It is for these reasons that I do not treat goodness as a necessary characteristic of God; cf. my "God and Goodness," in *Christian Faith and Philosophical Theology: Essays in Honour of Vincent Brümmer,* ed. G. van den Brink et al. (Kampen: Kok Pharos, 1992), pp. 244-48.

26. Cf. V. Brümmer's fundamental conviction in his *Theology and Philosophical Inquiry* (London: Macmillan, 1981), pp. 133-34. The term "ultimate" comes from Tillich's "Religion ist Richtung auf das Unbedingte," in *Religionsphilosophie* (Stuttgart: Kohlhammer, 1969[2]), p. 44.

Vedanta Hindus say that this reality is maya, that we generally do not see the actual reality, that the immutable lies in and behind the mutable, and that a brahmin is impersonal. Hindus of the bhakti schools say that the divine is personal, but at the same time is the deepest essence of all things. Believing Jews, Christians, and Muslims do not see God as the deepest essence of all things but rather as distinct from being: God is involved with human beings and the world. Therefore, on the basis of a comparison of concepts of God, one can say that some but not all religions worship the same God. From the Christian point of view there is still more to be said on this.

5.4 . . . No Other Gods before Me . . .

The consequence of the proposition that not all religions worship the same God is that quite a number of believers are mistaken in their worship. Do they worship idols? Is their belief of no value whatsoever? This conclusion does not follow from the above, as we will see in this section. I believe that people who do not know God in many cases still refer to God. I believe this view is justifiable on the basis of the Christian faith even though it may appear odd, since according to the psalmist the gods of the peoples were idols. In addition, the first of the Ten Commandments states: "You shall have no other gods before me."[27] The question now is whether Christians can say that some of those other believers worship the same God that Christians worship.

The biblical prophets fought constantly against idolatry, which was bound up with injustice. The gods were often local divinities, although these were also associated with higher gods. The worship of these divinities involved fertility cults and sometimes child sacrifice. Religion in this time and period was primarily polytheistic. The larger modern museums display ancient figures of the gods of the Philistines, Diana of

---

27. Deut. 5:7; Ps. 96:5; cf. §4.2 above. C. Burger, *Het Eerste Gebod: Verklaard door Laatmiddeleeuwse Theologen en door Maarten Luther* (Kampen: Kok, 1992), p. 29, points out that, in connection with religious pluralism, the first commandment must be justified absolutely. Cf. his "Gottesliebe, Erstes Gebot und Menschliche Autonomie bei spätmittelalterlichen Theologie und bei Martin Luther," *Zeitschrift für Theologie und Kirche* 89 (1992): 280-301.

the Ephesians, the images of the Greek and Roman gods. These vary in size, from huge statues taken from temples to tiny carvings that could be worn as amulets. The Old Testament depicts idolatry as going hand in hand with injustice and a lack of trust in God. For the present topic, one of the central and most discussed chapters of the Bible is Acts 17, which relates Paul's sermon in Athens on the Areopagus. It is a dramatic story, especially if one considers the situation: the marketplace is directly in front of the rocks of the Areopagus; a little to the right lies the Stoa, the philosophers' school; over his right shoulder Paul could see the Acropolis, the Athenian temple mountain with the Parthenon. Paul has seen altars throughout the entire city, which led him to the observation that people seek God by many paths. The author of Acts relates that Paul had even seen an altar to an unknown god. Paul did not conclude from the many idols that the people knew God; on the contrary, from the multiplicity of different images, he assumed that the people did not know God; in spite of all their religiosity they did not really know how things are ultimately. For this reason Paul preached the one God, the Creator of heaven and earth, and his revelation not in a stone image but in a human being, who lived and preached, who died, was buried, and on the third day rose again from the dead. Such preaching led to reactions of disbelief from most of the people in Athens. The relevant point here is that polytheism renders knowledge of God uncertain.

In chapter three I described the multiple aspects of the divine in the Hindu tradition, and that the divine unites opposite characteristics in itself, is inexhaustible, and ultimately is incomprehensible. All things are connected to the divine or even interrelated with it. The Bible distinguishes clearly between God and creation. Human projections of God are groundless, and the many gods and idols are sharply criticized. A person cuts down a tree and chops wood; he throws half of it in the fire, saying "ah, warmth," and carves and shapes the other half until it is his god and he says: "Save me, for you are my god!"[28] The critique of religion

---

28. Isa. 44:12-17. Cf. the second commandment: "You shall not make for yourself an idol in the form of anything in heaven above or on the earth beneath or in the waters below. You shall not bow down to them or worship them; for I, the Lord your God, am a jealous God" (Deut. 5:8-9). Cf. C. Link, "Das Bilderverbot als Kriterium theologischen Redens von Gott," *Zeitschrift für Theologie und Kirche* 74 (1977): 55-85, who stresses the following: God may not be depicted (or conceptualized) in such a way as to hold onto his presence; one may not mistake God for a

in the Bible is unmistakable. Religion comes under critique elsewhere as well — Socrates offered such a critique in Athens at the time that the temples on the Acropolis were built.[29] Critique of religion needs to be taken seriously; not all that glitters is gold. One of the most important elements in the critique of religion, certainly from a Christian point of view, is the societal use or abuse of religion. Christian faith is concerned with good and evil, justice and injustice. The issue of good and evil also played a significant role in the previous chapters. In chapter two, on Buddhism, I discussed the distinction between good and evil and the relativization of this distinction. In chapter three, on Hinduism, I examined the issue of justice and mercifulness; against this background I made critical comments on the ideas of karma and reincarnation. The discussion of Islam in chapter four revealed just how much Muslims are concerned about justice. On the issue of whether people *do* have a relationship with God in many religions — or, better yet, whether God has a relationship with other believers — one cannot ignore the critique of religion. There are indeed bad forms of religion; not every faith aspires to God.

The Bible, however, makes clear that there are people outside Israel and the church who believe in God.[30] Thus, from a biblical point

---

piece of the world or for the world; and one may not deify the cosmos (pp. 64-65). The Lord God is not without form, but because this form is never a given, the form of God is also *hidden* (p. 66), so that knowing God is never fully complete and is open historically and directed toward the future (pp. 76-80). Because God makes himself known within history in human experiences — that is, in Christ — the Christian faith concerns *hearing* the preaching of the gospel and not *seeing* divine images (pp. 72-74, 85-86) H. G. Geertsema, *Horen en Zien: Bouwstenen voor een Kentheorie* (Amsterdam: Free University Press, 1985), pp. 9, 14, 19, has indicated that where knowledge is based on *seeing*, it is directed toward that which is given, while knowledge that arises from *hearing* can view what is established as open and nondetermined.

29. For example, Plato, *Apology* (i.e., Socrates' apology), §15c, d, e.

30. Cf. B. Stoeckle, "De Buitenbijbelse Mensheid en de Wereldgodsdiensten," in *Mysterium Salutis,* 8, ed. J. Feiner and M. Löhrer, tr. O. Krops and T. de Meijer (Hilversum: P. Brand, 1968), p. 263, who, like Daniélou, speaks of "holy heathens." He indicates that according to the traditional view these are only exceptions. In this connection, Stoeckle speaks of "general revelation" that must be viewed as a continual activity of God (p. 266). As is well known, Karl Rahner spoke about anonymous Christians (see my *Religions and the Truth,* pp. 254-60, for an account with references), but, as noted in the section on exclusivism, one can replace the proposition "outside the church, no salvation" with the confession "outside Christ, no salvation." See also Runia, *Het Evangelie en de Vele Religies,* pp. 58-64.

of view, one must acknowledge that today there are people outside Judaism and the church who worship God — these people sometimes worship God more and have a more personal knowledge of him than many Christians do. I mean here people who worship God and not many gods at the same time, who do not add images of God as they please to what they find beautiful, but instead revere the Holy One and are sincere in what they say. That these people worship God is evident in the four attributes of "the same God": creative, willing, purposeful, and therefore personal. I do not think that this view conflicts with the command "you shall have no other gods before me or worship them."

But what of people who worship many gods? Or Buddhists who worship Amida Buddha and plead for his mercy? Or Zen Buddhists who strive for no-self and enlightenment? None of them intends to worship the one God, Creator of heaven and earth, since their ideas of God are irreconcilable with this concept. Is that all one can say? There are two sides to the coin: that of human beings, with our conscious and unconscious intentions, and that of God. If God's goodness is as great as it appeared in Jesus, would not God in his kindness have left some clue as to his nature for the millions of people who have not known and still do not know the gospel? The author of the book of Acts states that Paul has attributed to God the good that people have received in nature and in their lives: "In the past, he let all nations go their own way. Yet he has not left himself without testimony: he has shown kindness by giving you rain from heaven and crops in their seasons; he provides you with plenty of food and fills your hearts with joy."[31] Good, from mild rains to joy, comes from God — but not true insight? Not the feeling of connectedness to that which passes all understanding? It is the reality of God that lies behind the concepts of God and not the reality of, for example, the brahman. People may have the wrong concepts of God, but is then their entire faith — both the objective and the subjective side — misplaced? Or can elements of their faith, elements that they have received from God, but that they understand within the framework of their own religion, constitute true insight into reality and an actual bond with

---

31. Acts 14:16-17. According to D. C. Mulder, *Ontmoeting van Gelovigen* (Baarn: Bosch & Keuning, 1977), pp. 40, 43, God's closeness and care entail the basis for respect for other believers and working together with them — with the recognition that they have tasted and found something of God (p. 48).

God? If, as we have seen, religions do overlap in a number of places, then they have elements of truth. People partially know the truth, experience salvation, trust in God, or trust the fact that the good comes if they achieve no-self. As far as they experience true salvation, can it be anything but God's salvation?

Because false dilemmas have been posed, it is often presumed that people either experience salvation or they do not. It seems fairly obvious that many people in other religions and philosophies of life come to deep insights and experiences of salvation. But would the fact that they do not know the whole truth and do not experience complete salvation mean they have no insight and no salvation at all? Because "Eastern" salvation is a different salvation, does that mean that it is nothing at all? Salvation consists of a whole series of aspects — peace, inner calm, equanimity, harmonious living, justice and mercy, faith, hope, and love. Which Christian experiences all of this in its entirety? But if most Christians in this world have only a little bit of faith and salvation, would the heathens who do not know Christ yet have inner calm, peace, patience then not have a relationship with God? Would God really require people to confess specifically that they believe in Christ? And would God make an exception for baptized children with Down's syndrome (who often do not know much or even anything about God) but not for children of other believers who suffer from this syndrome? Nor for people who have trusted in their God and realized that they did not really know anything about God? I believe that Jesus' words apply here: "whoever is not against us is for us."[32] He refers to good deeds. The kingdom of God is wherever the Spirit of God inspires people and touches them in the depths of their soul — depths that at times are not understood by others or even by the people themselves. All that is good comes from God.

Here are two examples of texts that I feel cannot be rejected as idolatry nor seen as Christian. In the following Hindu poem, a prayer to Krishna, who does the poet seek other than God?

Children, wife, friend —
drops of water on heated sand.
I spent myself on them, forgetting you.
What are they to me now,

32. Mark 9:40. This text concerns people who cast out evil spirits.

154

O Mādhava, now that I am old and without hope,
apart from you. But you are the savior of the world
and full of mercy.
   Half my life I passed in sleep —
my youth, now my old age,
how much time.
I spent my youth in lust and dissipation.
I had no time to worship you.
   Ageless gods
have come and passed away.
Born from you, they enter you again
like waves into the sea.
For you have no beginning, and no end.
   Now
at the end, I fear
the messengers of Death.
Apart from you, there is no way.
I call you Lord,
the infinite and finite,
my salvation.[33]

The poet does not know God in Christ; he speaks of godly forms
born from the divine that then reenter the divine. God is distinct, a
being to whom one is able to pray, but at the same time he is like the
sea where streams once again mingle with its waters. This is an indication of how this concept of God differs from the biblical one. But
is it not particularly impressive how the poet trusts in God and prays
for nearness and mercy, since he does not know of God's love in
Christ? The Lord God can raise up children for Abraham from
stones;[34] if God desires it, would people who pray but use an incorrect
name and not know everything be unable to become his children?
   Another example: In the dialogue with Buddhist ideas the key
doctrines were those of good works and of justification. The point
was that there could be good works only if people had realized no-self.

---

33. Nibedan, "A Prayer to Krishna, the Finite and the Infinite, the Mighty
God," in *In Praise of Krishna: Songs from the Bengali,* tr. E. C. Dimock and D. Levertow
(Chicago: University of Chicago Press, 1967, reprint 1981), p. 69.
   34. Matt. 3:9.

Nevertheless, the Roman Catholic part of Christianity *traditionally* speaks of good works. Most Protestants do not feel that this is a reason to deny that Roman Catholics are Christians. But what is one to think of the thoughts of Ibn 'Ata'illah, a thirteenth-century Muslim?

> If you wish to be united with Him
> only after the cancellation of your sins
> and the wiping out of your arrogance,
> then you will never be united with Him!
> But if he wishes to unite Himself with you
> he covers your characteristics with His characteristics
> and cloaks your quality with His quality.
> And so he unites you with Himself
> due to that which comes to you from Him,
> not due to that which goes to Him from you.[35]

This does not sound like someone who believes he can attain salvation by upholding the law. Ibn 'Ata'illah does not appear to know of Christ in any way (other than through the Koran), yet does he not come close when he says "he covers your characteristics with His characteristics"? Has this Muslim worshiped an idol or given God companions? Or is the Hindu prayer I just quoted simply a misunderstanding and unbelief?

One disadvantage of this view is that one no longer knows precisely who does and who does not have a relationship with God. Is one here on a slippery slope, whereby first Muslims are included as believers, then theistic Hindus, and finally whoever else? If this is the case, then nearly every belief could be valid in the end. But that is not the point here. The point is that God is good, that people cannot verify what God does, and that one must respect that which others believe and the moments of truth they have discovered in their traditions. It is not necessary to have a clear criterion to determine which people have a relationship with God and which do not. There is no need to determine that or even to know that. To the disciples' question of how many will be saved, Jesus replies: "Make every effort to enter through the narrow

---

35. Ibn 'Ata'illah, *The Book of Wisdom,* tr. V. Danner; published with Ansari's *Intimate Conversations,* tr. W. M. Thackston (New York: Paulist, 1978), ch. 13, no. 130, p. 79.

door, because many, I tell you, will try to enter and will not be able to."[36] We do not have to verify the ins and outs of the heavenly accounts; they are in hands better than ours. But may we not acknowledge that God's attention goes beyond the church? That is why one can be certain of finding elements of truth and salvation beyond the scope of the Christian churches. The Spirit blows where it wills.

Jesus' answer, "make every effort to enter," has an entirely different point, one that implies a call for self-criticism. The Christian church has the gospel "at its disposal" and "knows" about the cross and resurrection. But what does that prove? How much has the Western church adapted to the Western economy and technology? Have not Western Christians become so individualized that the solidarity in the community is threatened? The encounter with the wisdom, courage, obedience in faith, and the relatedness with all things in other religions is thought-provoking. Consider also that the point of Karl Barth's fierce rejection of all forms of religion lay in his critique of Christianity. He saw religion as a human, self-willed attempt to justify and sanctify a concept of God developed for oneself,[37] which is why religion — Christianity included — is unbelief. Only because God's Word resounds in freedom is a person saved. The answer to the Word of God is not religion (the institution) but faith. Barth states that faith must arise again and again through the resounding of God's Word. There is much to be said for this, but I think that it may be taken one step further yet: the freedom of God's Word and Spirit is not restricted by the walls of the church.

This acknowledgment — that people who know Christ as well as those who do not know Christ can share in God's salvation, receive true insight, and live well — is not diminished by the special value of the gospel. The gospel goes deeper. That people without the gospel have also expressed deep insight into God's grace, into human abandonment of the self, and countless other things does not detract from the fact that the love and faithfulness of God has never come so clearly to light as in Jesus Christ. Free grace, accepting us as we are, justification through belief alone, which precedes good works — these are

36. Luke 13:24. Verse 27 indicates that the reason for the rejection lies in injustice. See Berkouwer, *Church*, p. 162.

37. K. Barth, *Church Dogmatics*, I/2, ed. G. Bromiley and T. F. Torrance, tr. G. T. Thomson and H. Knight (Edinburgh: T. & T. Clark, 1956), p. 280.

157

all insights that are of vital importance. The other side of the picture is also important: insight into the seriousness and depth of sin and the impossibility of self-justification and personal salvation apart from trust in and support from God. Recognition of the value of other religions does not diminish the importance of the Christian witness.

Two possible objections to the view presented in this book would, as far as I am concerned, carry a lot of weight if they were justified. The first is familiar from the discussion on the God of the Bible and the god of philosophers.[38] The objection is that Christians sometimes take part in long philosophical discussions on "God" before they make any reference to the Bible, so that the frameworks in which the biblical message will be heard are decided before reading the Bible. The church has followed this process for many centuries. Plato's influence can be traced already early in the church's history. The Middle Ages saw a development of a synthesis of Aristotelian philosophy and Christian belief. In the modern period Christianity threw in its lot with first Rationalism and later the Enlightenment. Thus a concept of God arose that was in fact far removed from the Bible — a supreme being that has become completely unbelievable. The Christian concept of God must be purified from philosophical accretions and the biblical stories must once again be heard. Parallel to this discussion one must ask whether the reasoning in this book suffers from the same defects as the reasoning concerning the god of the philosophers. Does a philosophical-religious concept of God take precedence, thus constituting the field in which room can still be found for the Bible? Does this lead to a relativization of the importance of the gospel for knowledge of God?[39]

38. Cf. de Boer, *De God van de Filosofen en de God van Pascal;* and the essays regarding his position in *De God van de Filosofen en de God van de Bijbel,* ed. H. M. Vroom (Zoetermeer: Meinema, 1991).

39. Cf. A. J. van der Bent, "Obstacles to the Inter-religious Dialogue," in *God so Loves the World: The Immaturity of World Christianity* (Maryknoll, N.Y.: Orbis, 1979), p. 39; Van der Bent, long-time librarian of the World Council of Churches, writes that the objection to dialogue within the World Council can be traced to two objections in particular: the fear of relativizing Christianity and the danger of syncretism. The objection to syncretism is described in detail by W. A. Visser 't Hoof, *No Other Name: The Choice between Syncretism and Christian Universalism* (London: SCM, 1963), pp. 9-82. That Christians can learn from others, however, does not imply syncretism; see my "Syncretism and Dialogue: A Philosophical Analysis," in *Dialogue and Syn-*

I have mentioned four closely related attributes of God that, if people acknowledge him as their "God," constitute sufficient grounds to speak of "the same God": creative, willing, purposeful, and (therefore) personal. One can say much about the way in which God is Creator. According to the school influenced by Barth, the Christian concept of creation is strongly determined by the historical experiences of Israel and much less or even scarcely so by nature.[40] Even though the Bible does not present any straightforward understanding of creation, it is certainly true that the concept of creation in the Koran differs from that in the Bible. One has only to think of the creation story in Genesis 1, which talks of the darkness and emptiness of the earth. Light and land are created from the chaos. But to say that the Bible depicts God as Creator in a different way than the Koran is not to say that Muslims do not know the Creator. It merely demonstrates, I believe, that they do not know God in the same way. The description of the attributes that people must ascribe to "their God" in order to acknowledge that they know God does not entail a concept of creation that has been fully worked out. The only aspect it concerns is the acknowledgment that this world has been purposely made by God. Therefore, this concept of "Creator" is not a mold that limits the room for the biblical (or Koranic) concept of creation but the greatest common denominator, namely, the acknowledgment that God made the world and that there is no other eternal power beside God — for example, the power of evil.[41] For this reason I do not accept as a valid objection the charge that the general concept of God is a mold into which the biblical concept must fit.

---

cretism, ed. J. D. Gort et al. (Grand Rapids: Eerdmans; Amsterdam: Rodopi, 1989), pp. 26-35. In my opinion the central question is whether the perception of the gospel is obscured by dialogue; hence the discussion of "the God of the Bible" and the *skandalon* of the cross.

40. E. J. Beker and K. Deurloo, *Het Begin in ons Midden: Aspecten van Bijbels Scheppingsgeloof* (Baarn: Ten Have, 1977).

41. Cf. J. van der Hoeven, "Schepping en Redding," in *De God van de Filosofen en de God van de Bijbel,* pp. 28-32, on the necessity of believing in God as the Creator. Although I would give many nuances to the concept of creation (largely in the line of Deurloo and de Boer; see nn. 38, 40 above), the sure expectation of the kingdom of God still presupposes the belief that there is not an evil, eternal power just as great as God, and hence the belief in God the Creator. Cf. the remarks on this topic by L. C. van den Brom, "En is Hij niet een God voor Filosofen?" in *De God van de Filosofen en de God van de Bijbel,* pp. 99-113.

A second serious objection that demands attention is that this view would leave no room for the *skandalon* of the cross,[42] that is, that the cross is an uncomfortable truth that people tend to avoid. We have seen that "the history of the cross" is a history of sin, unwillingness, injustice, God's faithfulness, faults of people, messages of prophets, and incomprehension. What is offensive is that people reject, stone, and crucify God's messengers, exploit the poor, do not feed the hungry, and crucify the last one sent by God, yet this Crucified One is the one God raised up from the dead. This is a scandal and an offense, a reason for not accepting the gospel. Acceptance of the gospel is impossible without self-criticism and confession of guilt. The question, therefore, is how one can acknowledge that other believers know God or else (unwittingly, in spite of incorrect concepts of God) have to do with God somehow without the *skandalon* playing a role. Here I look at a number of considerations.

First, something of the *skandalon* is found in other religious schools. The Islamic notion that has been mentioned states that a person is never without sin and that God's "quality" makes up for the shortage of human quality. Many contemplative schools suggest that one of the greatest dangers for the mystic is the belief that he or she is something, has achieved something, or even is able to achieve something. The condition for receiving salvation is often to give up believing in oneself.[43] The degree to which this insight is lacking makes it, in my opinion, more difficult to speak of the same God and of a deep relationship with God. So much depends on where precisely the *skandalon* of the gospel lies. The term stems from an expression of Paul: "Jews demand miraculous signs and Greeks look for wisdom, but we preach Christ crucified: a stumbling block to Jews and foolishness to Gentiles."[44] If one takes both elements together, the foolishness of and indignation aroused by the cross, then the *skandalon* of the gospel exists in the reversal of the order of "this world."[45] Good according to the rules is not always good; a person who

---

42. Cf. also H. Waldenfels, *Der Gekreuzigte und die Weltreligionen* (Zurich: Benziger, 1983), pp. 7, 9, 70-79.

43. See H. F. de Wit, *Contemplative Psychology,* tr. M. L. Baird (Pittsburgh: Duquesne University Press, 1991), p. 163.

44. 1 Cor. 1:22-23; cf. Gal. 5:11 ("the offense of the cross").

45. In John "the world" is the standard expression for the human world, which is full of darkness and hates Jesus. In contrast to this is the world of real life (for which one must be born again); cf. John 1:10; 7:7; 14:17; and others; see C. K. Barrett, *The Gospel According to St. John* (London: SPCK, 1978²), pp. 161-62.

has been successful according to the rules might well be degenerate. Faithfulness to the law is not everything — the central point is to love one's neighbor, as Jesus demonstrated by keeping company with publicans and sinners. Doing God's will does not always yield a knighthood; prophets got into all sorts of difficulties because of it and Jesus was crucified for it. The order of "this world" is not the order of God's kingdom. This implies an objection against a too strict observance of the halakah (the Jewish law), the *sharia* (the Islamic law), or the dharma. Another part of the *skandalon* of the cross is that it is concerned not with esoteric knowledge, a wisdom about that which lies beyond visible reality, but with trust in God in one's concrete life. In 1 Corinthians Paul is opposing a more or less gnostic school that also had representatives within the Christian community. This school had a negative view of earthly reality and was concerned with spiritual reality and wisdom. It distinguished between stronger people, those who had advanced further in such knowledge, and weaker people, and held that Christ, as a redeemed person, did not die on the cross. At bottom, each person has a spark of divine light, which people on the path to redemption had to follow.[46] In contrast to the esoteric school Paul emphasizes that knowledge passes and love remains, that Christ died on the cross, and the dead will be raised. Christian redemption does not involve the return of a person's divine spark to the divine, but rather a new *earth* with renewed people. This is also the reason why the resurrection is a *skandalon:* in spite of death God's hand will bring about new life on a new earth.[47] The *skandalon* of the cross and resurrection concerns this world in which sin rules and people depend on God's love and forgiveness, and it concerns the renewal of the world: a new earth.

I have taken up this offense of the gospel in previous chapters, particularly in the discussion of the no-self, the maya character of this world, and the emphasis on the meaning of the cross. We have seen that the other great traditions have also given offense; they also demand that people no longer fit neatly into "this world." Wherever

---

46. H. D. Wendland, *Die Briefe an die Korinther* (Göttingen: Vandenhoeck & Ruprecht, 1968), p. 161; cf. H. Jonas, *Gnostic Religion* (Boston: Beacon, 1958), pp. 42-47.

47. Cf. S. Samartha, "The Lordship of Jesus Christ and Religious Pluralism," in *Courage for Dialogue* (Geneva: WCC, 1981), pp. 93-94. In Acts 17:32 people listen to Paul's preaching until he begins to speak about the resurrection of the dead.

people in their religious traditions are helped to live in a truly humane way, to free themselves of wrong ties in "this world," and to live mercifully, justly, and lovingly, God may be seen in the background. This does not mean that the whole of a tradition can be said to be valuable or good. Traditions have valuable and bad elements: they help people to lead good lives and find salvation, but they can also often mislead people; they speak of the divine but also produce arbitrary concepts of God that are all too human — and thus the religious awareness in religious history is spoken of as *fabrica idolatorum* (factory of idols).[48] But is Christianity itself completely valuable and good?

5.5 Is Christianity Better?

Do these considerations now lead to the conclusion that Christianity is right and better than other religions? I do not think so. Christianity is not better than other religions. It is good and valuable insofar as it allows itself to be led by the gospel. Nevertheless, I would not like to speak of the *absoluteness of Christianity*. Christianity is not the highest religion but the religious tradition that at its best proclaims involvement with and love for people, which takes shape in a community of people and in diaconal care for those on the lowest rungs of society and those afflicted by disaster. At its worst Christianity collaborates with those in power, becomes involved in the structures of "this world," ignores neighborly love and repentance, and boasts about revelation as if it could control it. Christianity is good insofar as people actually believe in the God who revealed himself to Israel and became human in Jesus Christ, and allow the Spirit of God to guide them in their lives. *Real* Christian faith is good and true — I would say that it is better than other faiths because it is closer to life and reality (for reasons given in this book). Then it is a lived faith, both subjectively and objectively: not only subjective experiences or doctrinal expositions, but a lived, practical faith — experience, knowledge, and action together.

Christian faith that is badly understood is often worse than another faith. "Christianity" should produce much good, but the judgment of

---

48. J. H. Bavinck, *Religieus Besef en Christelijke Geloof* (Kampen: Kok, 1949), p. 188.

whether that is so is not easily answered. After all, good deeds are often not ones that attract a great deal of attention. To a large extent, Christian faith does not concern grand and "heroic" action but rather deeds of solidarity and faithfulness so small as to go unnoticed. Who can weigh the good fruits of the different religions against one another?[49] That judgment can better be left to God. People who know the gospel have a greater responsibility than people who do not, which is why poor and halfhearted Christianity is a very serious matter. For these same reasons the historical mistakes of Christian communities as well as the slowness to improve degrading conditions are so painful (consider slavery, racism, subordination of women, the poor in and around the large cities of Asia, Africa, and America). If one takes into consideration this heavy responsibility of Christianity on the basis of the knowledge of the gospel, it is impossible to call Christianity better. It is something else to say that the gospel is better because it testifies to unimagined events and passes on insights that reach deeper than other insights.

In this book I have given a number of the principal grounds for believing that genuine Christian faith is better than another faith. For me they are decisive. I do not claim to have a full understanding of the gospel nor to have realized all of its consequences, but I do think that I have articulated central notions of the gospel. Elaborate dogmatic explanations on Christology and the Trinity cannot be expected in a book such as this one. Such explanations would have to be a sober yet fervent doctrine of God, since we do not know much about God, about his thinking and being, other than that God's existence is a great mystery, what God is like, where he is, and how he acts: God lives in an impenetrable light. But we do know some central things, such as God has ministering hands, God is love and has accepted Jesus on the cross, and the Spirit of God works in and sustains this world, inspires and leads people — with or without their knowledge. Good Christian faith conserves the skepticism of the prophets and continues to observe life as it is lived. There are many things under the sun that biologists and doctors do not understand; reality is still much more complicated than can be established empirically. There is much that we do not know about God as well. But it does not concern knowing much; the point is knowing enough. A short psalm expresses this humility:

49. Cf. J. Hick, "The Non-Absolutism of Christianity," in *The Myth of Christian Uniqueness,* ed. Hick and P. R. Knitter (Maryknoll, N.Y.: Orbis, 1987), pp. 16-36.

My heart is not proud, O Lord,
my eyes are not haughty;
I do not concern myself with great matters
or things too wonderful for me.
But I have stilled and quieted my soul;
like a weaned child with its mother,
like a weaned child is my soul within me.
O Israel, put your hope in the Lord
both now and forevermore.[50]

The confession of the one God as Father, Son, and Spirit does not involve stating that which is too wonderful or examining the depths of God, but rather declaring that God is like a good father; that his love for people becomes clear in Jesus; that life involves love, peace, and justice; that God forgives sins; and that God works in the world through the Spirit to encourage, support, and inspire people. Christian spirituality is primarily living with trust in God and under the guidance of the Spirit of God, being thankful for mercy and inspired to live in accordance with the kingdom of God.

5.6 Critical Dialogue

I conclude with a few comments on dialogue. Critical dialogue entails a number of elements: a readiness to become acquainted with others in their individuality and to see their good sides, expressions of their own belief, a readiness to become acquainted with one another, and openness to mutual critical questions.[51] In this way dialogue goes hand in hand with individual development. Through the critical questions of others traditions can develop and adjust weak points. Religions have

---

50. Psalm 131.

51. See ch. 1 above. Cf. Mulder, *Ontmoeting van Gelovigen,* p. 49, on listening *critically* and differences of opinion. A description of a WCC consultation at Kandy (Sri Lanka, 1967): "Dialogue refers to any honest confrontation between adherents of different religions where the participants meet and challenge each other testifying to the depth of their experience to what stands forth as being of ultimate concern," in C. F. Hallencreutz, *New Approaches to Men of Other Faiths, 1938-1968: A Theological Discussion* (Geneva: WCC, 1970), p. 17.

gone through tremendous developments, and critical dialogue is one factor of that process. Dialogue with mutual critical questions is an old method of speaking about the truth. Because seeking the truth is foremost, it concerns the ball and not the players, it concerns attaining more insight in the truth and not who wins the discussion. The (pre)condition is that people learn from one another and be prepared to accept that one person can know something that another person does not. I think that this is possibly one of the greatest stumbling blocks for faith.

(a) People can learn from one another

Can one person have more insight than another? Does the personal character of faith not suggest that faith is purely personal and that one person does not know any better than another? I have made judgments between the gospel and a number of alternative religions, but is this legitimate? Can one tradition know more than another? There is not a single area in life where we exclude the possibility of one person knowing more than another. Modern society can exist only through specialization and the knowledge of things of which others have no idea. This pertains not only to technology and labor but also to daily life itself; one person can have more insight in solving human problems than another. Why should this be any different with regard to religion?

It is clear that one person can have more religious insight than another. This also holds true for morality (one person has a better sense of what can and must be done than another) and politics (even though everyone has the right to vote). If one person is able to know more than another, would it not also be possible for one religious tradition to know more than another? It would depend on whether something special has been experienced and whether experience has been gained together. People who have experienced things that do not happen to everyone have something to tell others, and this also holds for religious traditions. A way of life might be found that stimulates tranquillity and wisdom, and limits or even eliminates greed — through meditation, for example. Such a way of life is maintained by a community; people stimulate one another, tell one another how things should or should not be done, and how things can be done better. Religious ways of life are handed down by groups of people. One group can have insights and habits that others (severely) lack. Another possibility is that people experience things that are not witnessed by or do not occur to others, and insights are derived from this. If this occurs, then those people are witnesses of what they have experienced. Thus Jews witness about the oneness of God and their history with God. Christians also witness about Jesus of Nazareth. The apostles experienced things that they passed on to others and that are written in the New Testament. People have believed this, experienced it in their faith, and are able to witness about it.[52] Muhammad has also testified to the oneness, greatness, and mercifulness of God. In principle, there is not a single reason why the great witnesses would not really have something to say. One religious tradition can pass on more insight than another — which does not say that all believers appropriate and use (or neglect) the deep insights of their tradition.

It seems to me that no sensible person can deny that one tradition is able to pass on insights from which much can be learned by another tradition. Particularly good representatives of a religion are able to pass such insights on. Why else would people continue to talk about Gandhi, the Dalai Lama, or John XXIII? Some people embody actual aspects of their tradition. I think that in the earlier chapters of this book, where I made judgments on Buddhism, Hinduism, Islam, and Christianity, it is clear that the great traditions are able to learn from one another. Buddhism has much to offer with respect to the internalization and equanimity encouraged in meditation, detachment, the relativization of the self and of individual merit, and the concern with nature. The great points of Hinduism are the relatedness with all things, the acceptance of the place and task of the individual in the community, a sense for the closeness of the divinity, and the fostering of personal virtue, just to mention a few points. Islam is inspiring in its seriousness with respect to the religious tradition and obedience, and the willingness to place the whole of life under the authority of God's commandments. The prop-

---

52. Cf. Samartha, *Courage for Dialogue,* p. 103: "Christians believe that in Jesus Christ the Ultimate has become intimate with humanity, that nowhere else is the victory over suffering and death manifested so decisively as in the death and resurrection of Jesus Christ, and that they are called upon to share this good news humbly with their neighbours."

osition that one tradition can pass on insight that another tradition lacks obtains again and again. As I have indicated above at more length, I reject the strategy of posing false dilemmas. That applies also on this point. It is not the case that one tradition possesses deep insight and knowledge of everything while another tradition does not. On the contrary, that one tradition knows a deeper truth than another allows for the possibility of true insight in the other tradition that the first tradition does not have. Traditions can learn from one another. One side effect is that, in the encounter with other believers or with the critique of religion, one rediscovers a depth in one's own tradition that had apparently been forgotten.

(b) The nature of dialogue

Much has been published in the area of interreligious dialogue, but there are strong differences of opinion on the nature and aim of dialogue. In the *Guidelines* for dialogue, drawn up by the Department for Dialogue of the World Council of Churches at the time, dialogue is described as a fundamental part of Christian service in the community and an expression of neighborly love.[53] Dialogue should not be a matter of doctrinal disputes, since dialogue is more concerned with people of another faith than with a theoretical, impersonal system of faith. Dialogue may take place anywhere: within the family, on the street, at work, or between representatives of religious groups. The *Guidelines* posits that dialogue cannot be clearly defined — it is a way of life. This document makes several comments in relation to openness to the thinking of others, acceptance of the cultural background of others, and so on. Thus the *Guidelines* stresses the great importance of dialogue between people with different convictions for the purpose of peace in the community. The most important aim of dialogue is to seek fellowship together.[54]

53. *Guidelines on Dialogue with People of Living Faiths and Ideologies* (Geneva: WCC, 1979, 1982²), pp. 10-11. For the development of thought on other believers within the WCC, see Hallencreutz, *New Approaches;* on the development within the department for dialogue of the WCC (1971-1991), see D. C. Mulder, "A History of the Sub-unit on Dialogue of the World Council of Churches," *SID* 2 (1992): 135-51.

54. W. Ariarajah, "The Understanding and Practice of Dialogue: Its Nature, Purpose and Variations," in *Faith in the Midst of Faiths* (Geneva: WCC, 1977), p. 57.

Mutual understanding is often seen as an aim of dialogue.[55] But if mutual understanding is a condition for a peaceful and just community, then so is the understanding of the content of faith of others. One cannot understand a Hindu as a Hindu if one does not know something of Hindu tradition. In order to understand someone personally, one must also pay close attention to the way in which that person understands her or his tradition. Every encounter has a subjective side as well as an objective side. If one considers someone's personal experience more important in some situations, then one places religious organizations and systems of doctrine in the background. When Muslims or others speak with Christians about practical problems (such as the possibility of bringing religious habits into practice in European countries and North America), then the practical issues are in the foreground. But even in such practical issues, the content of faith plays a role and thus may not be neglected.

One can distinguish three aspects in dialogue: knowledge, the experience of faith, and sociopolitical matters.[56] These three aspects cannot be separated, although, as the context requires, the discussion will concern one aspect more than the others. Discussion on the content of faith may not be omitted. Ultimately, faith can be taken seriously only if one also considers what is true, and this is why discussion of what people believe is vital. Of course, a discussion on the content of faith should not be a doctrinal skirmish. I hope I have made clear that in such a discussion the experiential side of faith should be very important: one must try to see the strong point in other faiths, and that there may be critical questions again and again. Such a discussion also has room for a mutual witness as to what one believes.[57] Only when one believes that the gospel depicts life in all

55. In, for example, Aloysius Berchmans Chang, "The Spirituality of Dialogue," *Bulletin of the Secretariatus pro non-Christianos* 17 (1982): 251 ("one of the main results"); Masao Abe, "Zen as Self-Awakening," *Japanese Religions* 8 (1975): 25 ("real and creative mutual understanding").

56. L. de Silva, "The Understanding and Goal of Dialogue," *Dialogue* 4, nos. 1-2 (1977): 3-4.

57. Cf. Paolo Marella (at the time president of the Secretariat for Non-Christians in the Vatican) summarizes the official stance of the Roman Catholic Church as *"mission in the spirit of dialogue,"* "Nature, Presuppositions and Limits of the Dialogue with Non-Christians," *Bulletin* 4 (1969): 9. Dialogue serves a broader purpose than simply mission: understanding, community, brother- and sisterhood and unity in the "human

its depths can one hope that others will also learn to see things with the eyes of the gospel and that other traditions and cultures — as A. Camps puts it — are "infected" with the ideals of Jesus Christ.[58] All the main religions have undergone enormous developments in the course of centuries and contain within themselves very different traditions. Critical dialogue can play a large role in the further development of religions in that followers are challenged to face the weaknesses of their (interpretation of their) religion and to improve on them.

We have seen that religion provides people with a picture of life as it should be. One can call this a normative depiction of human beings. Religions provide values and norms. In a community with many religious and philosophical traditions side by side, it is inevitable that people appropriate various idealized concepts. The preceding chapters have shown again and again how much religion can influence life. For this reason dialogue among followers of various religions and philosophies is one of the most urgent tasks of our time. Through technical and economic developments people have (even) more dealings with one another than before. We must be able to live together. The urgency of this issue has been captured in the title of a collection of essays: *Death or Dialogue*.[59] The alternative to clashes and conflicts between religious groups is an open, sensitive, yet critical discussion. This is meaningful not only for people who believe but also for the

---

family," p. 10. Cf. also A. Wessels, "Dialoog of Getuigenis?" in *De Dialoog Kritisch Bezien,* ed. A. W. Musschenga (Baarn: Ten Have, 1983), pp. 153-71; and Mulder, *Ontmoeting met Gelovigen,* pp. 53-56.

58. A. Camps, *De Weg, de Paden and de Wegen* (Baarn: Bosch en Keuning, 1977), p. 8 (the English translation, *Partners in Dialogue: Christianity and Other World Religions,* tr. John Drury [Maryknoll, N.Y.: Orbis, 1983], omits this remark). Cf. his farewell address, *Het Derde Oog: Van een Theologie in Azië naar een Aziatische Theologie* (Nijmegen: Catholic University of Nijmegen, 1990).

59. L. Swidler et al., eds., *Death or Dialogue? From the Age of Monologue to the Age of Dialogue* (London: SCM, 1990), p. vii. A host of other literature, on dialogue as well as examples of dialogues, includes: O. C. Thomas, ed., *Attitudes Toward Other Religions* (London: SCM, 1990); P. F. Knitter, *No Other Name? A Critical Survey of Christian Attitudes Toward the World Religions* (Maryknoll, N.Y.: Orbis, 1986[2]); A. Race, *Christians and Religious Pluralism: Patterns in the Christian Theology of Religions* (London: SCM, 1983); K. Cracknell, *Towards a New Relationship: Christians and People of Other Faith* (London: Epworth, 1986); L. Swidler, ed., *Toward a Universal Theology of Religion* (Maryknoll, N.Y.: Orbis, 1987); G. D'Costa, ed., *Christian Uniqueness Reconsidered* (Maryknoll, N.Y.: Orbis, 1990).

community as a whole. Religions contribute much to a satisfactory and responsible community, but they can also do much harm to the community, which is why public dialogue must be part of urgent social statements.

(c) Criteria for critical dialogue

The last two questions I would like to address concern the rationality of critical dialogue. What are the actual criteria for dialogue? If there are no neutral criteria, then how is *critical* dialogue possible? Then there is still the question of what force a partial justification of faith such as the one offered in this book has if there are no neutral standards by which differences of opinion may be settled.

Literature in the area of philosophy of religion presents criteria for the judgment of religious claims to truth. I have presented and discussed a series of criteria elsewhere.[60] Some people claim that all criteria by which a religion can be gauged are internal to the religion, thereby permitting only an internal testing, which leads to the incomparability of religious traditions. I have rejected this view in previous sections, as well as demonstrated that it is possible to partially understand other traditions; this implies that there are questions that others can answer, and makes a critical dialogue possible. The opposite view is that criteria can be established from a neutral standpoint by which all religious insights can be tested. This view, however, overlooks the fact that religion demands a transformation: people must be converted, learn to look at things differently, learn to see everything in obedience to God, and so on. The implication is that religious insights can be properly understood only if one does not view them from a distance, but masters them and appropriates them personally. The outcome of all of this is that it is impossible for religious insights to be tested in a neutral manner, the reasons for this lying in first, the encompassing and properly basic character of religion; second, the conversion or change in thinking that religions demand; and third, the qualifications of the use of religious language.[61]

60. See my *Religions and the Truth,* pp. 359-75.
61. Glyn Richards, after discussing criteria, concludes that something can be said about religious assertion on factual issues and the consistency of doctrine, but

In the meantime a number of demands can be made for religious insights, but they only assist in separating the wheat from the chaff. Five such indications of religious insights can be found in the great traditions: (1) religious insight must deal with transcendence, (2) religious insight must integrate experiences (on the basis of which one strives for consistency and coherence), (3) religious insight must have universal validity, (4) religious insight must aid the person in becoming a true person, and (5) religious insight must be based in fundamental human experiences. I have simply given a summary of these criteria here, without giving them further foundation and expounding on them.[62] On the basis of these criteria one cannot determine who is right, but it is possible to see whether a religious tradition can be taken seriously as a genuine tradition. It is already significant to be able to separate the wheat from the chaff. Not only that, these minimum requirements make possible a meaningful discussion between followers of different religions.

Within Christianity in particular a number of people have proposed accepting the practice of religion as a criterion for good faith: by their fruits they shall be known! *Liberation* in particular has been considered: good religion aids in liberating people. Then the evangelical preference for the poor would provide the correct general context in which dialogue can be meaningfully established. But choosing for the poor is not a failsafe criterion for forming judgments; rather it is a point of departure that must be further clarified in dialogue.[63] Through mutual involvement in the process of liberation people would learn to understand one another better. Dialogue consists of this liberating praxis; from this point it is possible to communicate about doctrine. Christians can only work together with those who think differently if they serve salvation (or, in Christian terminology, the kingdom of God).[64] It appears to me

---

that there is no criterion independent of tradition to settle the controversial claims to truth. He posits justly "that the question for an independent criterion of truth is even confused and is based on an error" (*Toward a Theology of Religions* [London: Routledge, 1989], pp. 117-18); see my *Religions and the Truth,* p. 370.

62. See my *Religions and the Truth,* pp. 361-70.

63. P. F. Knitter, "Toward a Liberation Theology of Religions," in *Myth of Christian Uniqueness,* ed. Hick and Knitter, p. 186. Cf. also Knitter, *No Other Name?* p. 231.

64. Knitter, "Toward a Liberation Theology of Religions," p. 187. J. D. Gort, "Liberative Ecumenism: Gateway to the Sharing of Religious Experience," in *On*

that it is precisely this prophetic element that is of utmost importance for the Christian tradition and a few other traditions. As we saw in chapters two and three of this book, however, it appears that the Buddhist and Hindu traditions differ from the Christian tradition on this point. Not everybody understands salvation to mean the same thing. Not every religious school is directed toward salvation on earth. This does not exclude overlappings in the idea of salvation, but it makes it difficult to work with a specific Christian goal as the perspective from which dialogue can be conducted. The answers to questions of salvation among the religions differ from and sometimes even exclude one another, with the result that the process of liberation is viewed differently.[65] Practical criteria do not help to settle the claim to truth, because generally they must be formulated so vaguely that almost all religions fulfill them to some degree; and as soon as one becomes more concrete, opinions differ.[66] In short, verification through practice does not yield all that much, which is the reason for the plea for an open, sympathetic, and critical dialogue, paying attention to religious experience and the consequences of religion in practical life.

Finally, there is the question of what kind of persuasive power the considerations such as those made in this book have. Dialogue with those who think differently is done by someone who already has her or his own insights. Does one simply judge other people's faith in terms of one's own tradition? Is the fact that there are no neutral criteria nor any rationale for proving the truth of belief not a serious

---

Sharing Religious Experience, ed. J. D. Gort et al. (Amsterdam: Rodopi; Grand Rapids: Eerdmans, 1992), p. 102; Gort is similarly optimistic: the opening for dialogue lies in common action with respect to the poor. See J. Verkuyl, "The Biblical Notion of the Kingdom: Test of Validity for Theology of Religion," in *The Good News of the Kingdom,* ed. Charles Van Eugen et al. (Maryknoll, N.Y.: Orbis, 1993), pp. 71-81.

65. See D. C. Mulder, "Alle Geloven op Één Kussen? Over de Religieuze Basis van de Interreligieuze Dialoog," in *Religies in Nieuw Perspectief: Opstellen Aangeboden aan D. C. Mulder* (Kampen: Kok, 1985), p. 147.

66. Other problems in verification in praxis are that the actual practice always deviates from what was planned, the judgment of the practice itself demands interpretation and theory, the conclusion of effect from cause is not compulsory (certainly not if religious instructions for action overlap); see my "Right Conduct as a Criterion for True Religion," in *Models and Criteria of Interreligious Relations,* ed. J. Kellenberger (London: Macmillan, 1993), pp. 106-31, for a summary and extensive discussion.

obstacle? With these objections in mind I would like to ask who would have thought that, after so many centuries of people living in various traditions, religious pluralism could be dissolved by a few decades of study and encounter among different believers. One can see that the entire Western philosophy also breaks up into a plurality of schools: there is no *one* philosophy. It was naive of Enlightenment theology to think that a so-called natural religion could be developed that would overcome the religious differences and make the actual religions superfluous. There is a plurality of cultures, each having their own conceptions of what being good entails, the nature of transcendence, and what position people must hold in society. Neutral ground does not exist; everyone has a philosophy.

The only way to deal with the differences is to discuss them, study them, think about them, pose critical questions, give answers to questions, and learn from one another. This must be a *public debate:* whoever wishes to speak may do so. A condition is that one must take the trouble to acquire a profound knowledge of the ideas of others and that one must also deal with critical questions directly. The problem with public debate on philosophy is that religion has a strong personal nature — something that one must keep in mind. Yet, by way of questioning, one can still formulate a critique to which other parties can respond and ask questions in turn. Experience shows that with the passage of time people can learn to understand each other better. In a world of ethnic and religious twists, that in itself is already a great achievement. People can learn from one another without converting to another religion — although conversion is not excluded, since in critical dialogue people may come to think radically differently. Even when a Christian hopes that another will see more of the truth of the gospel, she opens herself to that which is valuable in other traditions and thereby exposes herself to other influences. Some Christians appropriate practices or thoughts of others or are influenced by them; sometimes people lose their old faith and arrive at another insight; still others lose all faith. Because faith is anchored deeply in human experience, these changes are usually lengthy processes; faith seldom changes during a discussion. The possibility of arriving at another insight, however, is not an argument against critical dialogue. One may lose faith in more ways than one — the most obvious being by not practicing the faith, not thinking about it, and not discussing it. Dialogue can stimulate one to concentrate on the heart of the gospel. Why should one evade the critical questions? Truth lasts the longest.

Critical dialogue with those of another faith, those who think differently, and also with religious critics involves deepening the insight in truth by learning from one another. Christianity itself has learned much from other traditions in the course of centuries. In this way religious and philosophical schools in a culture are able to interact and challenge one another to face real questions and problems. The interpretation of holy books may change as well, just as the interpretation of the Bible itself has undergone developments throughout the centuries. Gandhi interpreted the Bhagavad Gita in a new way.[67] Various interpretations of the Koran are also proposed. People can influence one another in ways such as this, since in a real dialogue one does not remain unchanged. Dialogue is not expected to decrease the number of religions, but it is hoped that dialogue and encounter will soften the tensions in society and help people to work toward a peaceful and just life together. Moreover, whoever believes that God is most truly revealed in Christ may also hope that others can understand it and will possibly also learn to see this truth. All sympathetic and critical speaking and reading is ultimately sustained by the desire to gain, together with others, more insight into life and the great connections in which life exists in order to live out of this insight.

67. See R. Fernhout, "Combatting the Enemy: The Use of Scripture in Gandhi and Godse," in *Human Rights and Religious Values,* pp. 120-32.